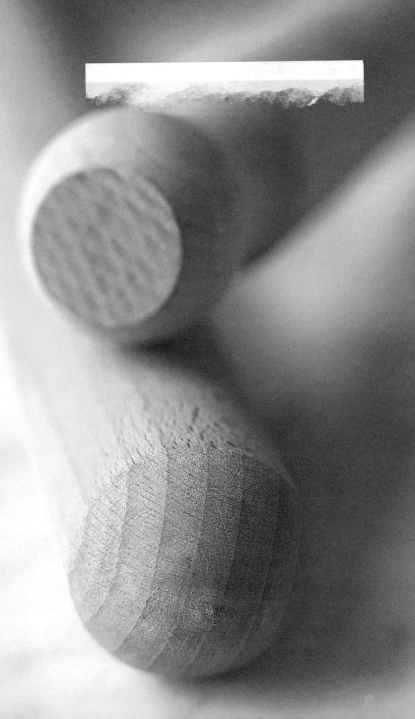

TARTS
SWEET AND SAVORY

TARTS
SWEET AND SAVORY

MAXINE CLARK
PHOTOGRAPHY BY MARTIN BRIGDALE

RYLAND
PETERS
& SMALL

LONDON NEW YORK

Dedicated to my sister Jacks, my
friend, who is known to make a
decent tart or two, and is a constant
source of inspiration.

First published in the United States in 2003
by Ryland Peters & Small, Inc.
519 Broadway, 5th Floor
New York, NY 10012
www.rylandpeters.com

10 9 8 7 6 5 4 3 2 1

Text © Maxine Clark 2003
Design and photographs
© Ryland Peters & Small 2003

Printed in China

Library of Congress Cataloging-in-Publication
Data

Clark, Maxine.
  Tarts : sweet and savory / Maxine Clark :
photography by Martin Brigdale.
    p. cm.
  ISBN 1-84172-420-3
  1. Pies. I. Title.
TX773 .C565 2003
641.8'652–dc21

2002014224

Senior Designer Steve Painter
Commissioning Editor Elsa Petersen-Schepelern
Editor Kim Davies
US Editor Helen Martineau
Production Meryl Silbert
Art Director Gabriella Le Grazie
Publishing Director Alison Starling

Food Stylists Maxine Clark, Linda Tubby
Stylist Helen Trent
Indexer Hilary Bird

Author's acknowledgments

Thanks to all those listed below for helping to
create this beautiful book.

Elsa, for asking me to do this book and being
a kindly dragon where necessary.

Kim, for her good-humored, efficient editing.

Steve for his elegant design and calm control
during photography, and his great taste in tarts!

Martin for his luscious, light, atmospheric
photography and his relish for a good tart!

Helen for her simply spectacular styling and
boundless enthusiasm.

And Becca Hetherston, without whose good-
humored assistance in all things tarty at the
studio, I could not have managed.

Notes

All spoon measurements are level unless
otherwise specified.

All eggs are large, unless otherwise specified.
Uncooked or partially cooked eggs should not
be served to the very young, the very old,
those with compromised immune systems,
or to pregnant women.

Before baking, weigh or measure all ingredients
exactly and prepare baking pans or sheets.

Ovens should be preheated to the specified
temperature. Recipes in this book were
tested in several kinds of oven—all work
slightly differently. I recommend using an
oven thermometer and consulting the
maker's handbook for special instructions.

contents

home is where the tart is ...

I just love making tarts, and have done so ever since watching my grandmother baking us little tarts when we came home from school and letting us fill them with lemon curd. But then it's in the genes, you see: I come from a family of bakers and I am Scottish (we love to bake). Making your own pastry dough well is one of the simple pleasures in life. Your own pastry bears no resemblance to the bought stuff in either taste or texture, AND you can monitor the ingredients. Ready-made dough containing real butter is almost impossible to find these days—the result is pastry with no flavor and a colorless appearance. Whatever fat you use, it must be pure, and your flour good quality. Good ingredients make great dishes!

Tarts are faster and much less complicated to make than pies, as they are not covered. They can be rustled up at a moment's notice, even if you haven't made the dough already (try to make batches and divide into useful amounts to thaw later). Don't be scared to make your own pastry—with modern appliances such as the food processor, bad pastry is a thing of the past. Don't be put off buying ready-made pastry if it encourages you to become a tart-maker!

The majority of tarts in this book are sweet—it naturally worked out that way— but there are recipes for everyday tarts, tarts for a special occasion, classic tarts, and comfortingly self-indulgent tarts. People notice when they bite into a homemade crust, revealing a heavenly interior, so come to grips with pie-crust-making and you'll never look back. Like baking your own bread, it is a very satisfying and rewarding experience. Go ahead and tackle a tart today!

basics

equipment and utensils

For dough-making

A large **work surface** (a marble slab if you are lucky, but make sure it is big enough) is essential for making a tart. Never roll out dough in a cramped area or you will risk rolling unevenly or stretching the dough. The surface should be cool (not next to the stove) to prevent the dough from becoming soft and unmanageable.

Accurate **weighing scales** or measuring cups to get the quantities and proportions correct.

Measuring spoons for accurate measuring—necessary with all baking. Recipes in this book require all measurements to be level.

Large and small heatproof **measuring cups**. They are dual purpose—for accurate measurement as well as suitability for the microwave (which I use as a kitchen tool like all other equipment).

Fine and medium **strainers** are essential to sift and aerate flour and remove lumps, making for a lighter pastry. Confectioners' sugar should ALWAYS be sifted through a fine mesh—the lumps will never beat out.

Assorted **mixing bowls**—I find I use light plastic bowls or wide stainless steel ones for dough-making, but glass or Pyrex are perfectly suitable. The important thing is to make sure the bowl is big enough for the job—you want plenty of room to move for your hands and the ingredients when rubbing in. This, too, aerates the dough.

A **food processor** is a MUST if you have hot hands, or if you think you can't make pastry! It removes all the fear of butter melting into the flour, because it mixes fat and flour so quickly and evenly. Just remember to pulse the machine when adding liquids so that the dough will not be overworked and become tough.

A **flour sifter/shaker** is not absolutely necessary, but it does stop you from adding too much extra flour to the work surface or dough. Too much extra flour destroys the proportions and affects taste and texture.

Several **pastry brushes**, so you always have a dry one on hand for brushing excess flour off the dough and one for brushing liquids and glazes.

A **pastry scraper** for scraping the dough off a work surface and for cleaning off all the messy bits. Indispensable.

A **spatula** can be used instead, but is best used for chopping in the flour in French pastries such as pâte brisée (page 24).

Microplane graters were a revelation to me, and once acquired, you'll wonder how you ever lived without them. There are three grades—fine, medium, and coarse. Fine is perfect for grating lemons, nutmeg, garlic, ginger, and Parmesan. Medium for other cheeses, and general grating. Coarse is perfect for grating butter into pastry dough or grating streusel dough (page 115).

A **pastry blender** is something I have only used occasionally, but some cooks swear by it. It is a series of thin metal loops connected to a handle, which you use to cut the fat into the flour. It prevents "hot hand syndrome" and aerates the dough. I prefer to use an old round-bladed cutlery knife (or two—one in each hand) to cut in the fat.

All-purpose **plastic wrap or plastic bags** are absolutely necessary to wrap dough before chilling or freezing, protecting it, and preventing it from drying out.

Always keep a bottle of **ice water** in the refrigerator so you have chilled water on hand for dough-making.

Choosing tart pans

Good solid **baking sheets** that won't buckle in the oven are ESSENTIAL—really good ones cost a fortune, but they soon become part of the family!

A selection of sizes of **tart pans** with false bottoms—the heavier the better, so they won't buckle. Heavy pans will cook tarts more evenly. It is always worth spending extra money on a few very good pans rather than buying a lot of cheap ones that will warp. (I don't recommend china or glass dishes for baking tarts as they give the dreaded "soggy bottom.") Traditionally, fluted edges designated sweet fillings while plain edges indicated a savory filling. The most useful sizes are 8, 9, and 10 inches and sometimes a 12-inch for a crowd.

Some people prefer **flan rings** to set on a baking sheet, instead of the false-bottom pans. These are the chef's choice as they

are strong and easy to store. The most useful are 8, 9, and 10 inches.

A **tarte tatin pan** is a luxury, but worth having if this is your favorite tart! It is a heavy pan specially designed to conduct the heat well to caramelize the apples without burning. Two sizes are useful— 8 and 11 inches.

Metal or enamel **pie plates** with a wide rim to take a good crust—both deep and shallow—are essential for traditional American tarts and pies, and tarts that need a decorative edge such as treacle tart. I use 8 to 9 inches.

Assorted **springform pans** are great for deeper tarts, as they are easy to remove once the tart is cooked. The most useful are 8, 9, and 10 inches.

Tartlet pans in various sizes and shapes. I collect them, but find the most useful are false-bottom—4 inches for individual tarts and 2½–3 inches for tartlets.

Patty pans are the traditional pans for making little tartlets in bulk, like curd or jam tarts.

Mini-muffin pans are wonderful for making cocktail-size tartlets in bulk and little phyllo tartlets.

Rolling out and lining the pan

Ruler—a must for checking pan sizes and drawing or cutting straight edges when decorating the dough.

Long straight **rolling pin** (wooden or nylon) with no handles. I find that handles spoil the even rolling action. Keep your rolling pin somewhere where the surface won't be damaged by other kitchen utensils (not in the utensil drawer!) If using a rolling pin to smash or pound, use the end, not the long surface that will become pitted and will transfer marks onto the dough.

A very sharp **cook's knife** or thin-bladed filleting knife for trimming the pastry—it

must be razor-sharp to cut through the dough without dragging it.

Large **serrated knife** for trimming and slicing—this stays nice and sharp and is good for cutting baked pie crusts.

A **fork** for pricking tart bases and decorating.

Assorted sizes of **spatulas**—I have three sizes, and I use all of them equally at different times. A large one will help to loosen rolled-out dough from the work surface, a small one will lift little dough circles into a tart pan and a tiny one will lift pastry decorations onto the tart edge.

Plastic wrap, wax paper, aluminum foil, and **nonstick parchment paper**, for wrapping dough, lining pans, and for baking blind. Note: parchment paper and wax paper are completely different things; one is nonstick and the other just impervious to grease.

Ceramic or metal **baking beans**, or just a container of rice or dried beans that can be used over and over again for baking blind. I use all sorts of things to weigh down the dough when baking blind (page 19). It depends on what's in the pantry and on the size of the tart. Little ones can be filled with rice or lentils, larger ones with dried beans, peas, pasta, or a mixture.

Assorted **cookie cutters**, both plain and fluted, to cut out small tarts to line tartlet pans, muffin pans, or mini-muffin pans.

Decorating pastry

Cookie cutters of all types. You can create dozens of decorative edges using leaf cutters, shaped cutters—even animals, to customize your tarts. I am forever adding to my collection.

Pastry wheels make short work of cutting straight lines and give decorative edges.

A **small sharp knife** will help to cut patterns on decorations.

A **lattice cutter** is a clever way of making a professional-looking lattice top for tarts and pies. It cuts out a lattice, which can be opened up like a web to drape over a tart. However, it does lack the homemade look.

Baking and cooling tarts

An **electronic timer** is one of my most essential pieces of equipment. You cannot possibly cook pastry and not burn it without one!

Oven gloves—a must, no damp dish towels to burn your hands!

Wire or metal **cooling racks**—assorted sizes, 1 large and 2 medium.

Mesh cloches/domes are very useful for protecting the tart against damage as it cools, letting the air circulate freely.

A large **cake-lifter** will help to lift the tart onto a plate without it falling to bits.

A **serrated spatula** is useful to slice the tart then serve it or lift it onto a plate.

A word about microwaves

All microwaves differ in power output, so be guided by the maker's handbook. The times given here are only guidelines—you must get to know your own microwave.

A word about convection ovens

Most must usually be set 20°F lower than regular ovens. Consult the maker's handbook. This is important when baking.

Care of equipment

All metal pans should be washed gently in warm soapy water, rinsed, and dried thoroughly (in the turned off oven after baking), or they will rust.

Some pans just need a wipe with paper towels—doing this will gradually build up a nonstick patina on the pan, making it look well-used and giving it character.

top tart tips

- Water/liquid quantities are never exact, as there are so many variables. A rule of thumb is to add slightly less than is stated, as you can always add more—but too much and the dough is lost!

- Always have a dry pastry brush on hand to remove excess flour.

- If your hands are sticky with dough, stop everything and wash them, then dry them and dust with flour—this will stop the dough from sticking to them and prevent horrible dry flaky bits falling off your hands into the dough when you roll it out!

- Try to flour your hands and the rolling pin rather than bathing the dough in flour to prevent sticking.

- When rolling dough, keep it moving on a "hovercraft" of flour and it will never stick.

- Rolling dough directly on a piece of nonstick parchment paper or plastic wrap will mean it can be moved around easily and will not stick to the work surface!

- Always roll directly away from you and move the dough round by short turns in one direction so that you roll it evenly.

- Setting two chopsticks (or similar) on either side of a dough before you roll it out will help you to roll it out evenly to the thickness of the chopstick and no less.

- If you are a beginner, don't try to roll out the dough too thinly—just cook it for a bit longer when you bake it blind (page 19).

- There is no need to grease a pan before lining. All dough has fat in it and will in effect be nonstick. It is the filling leaking out over the edges or through holes that makes dough stick.

- When you line a tart pan, try rolling the flour-dusted dough around the rolling pin to help you to pick it up—this will avoid stretching the dough and stop it from shrinking when cooking.

- Use a small piece of extra dough wrapped in a piece of plastic wrap to help to push the dough into the edges of the pan. Once this is done you can press the dough up the sides of the pan and cut off the overhang with a very sharp knife. I like to press the dough again into the flutes of the ring after cutting off the excess to give a good shape.

- If in doubt, CHILL! CHILL! CHILL! Raw dough will benefit from thorough chilling at every stage—I like to freeze dough-lined pans before baking blind as this really sets the dough so it holds its shape. Freeze the unbaked pie crust after lining the pan with dough, even just for 15 minutes. This gives the dough a good rest and makes the tart easy to line with foil and beans when baking blind. Work quickly, and get it into the oven before it thaws, and you will have a perfect pie crust!

- ALWAYS chill a double crust pie before baking.

- Always glaze then chill a pie before making any marks on the dough.

- Always chill a pie before making slits in the dough.

- Always put a tart on a baking sheet before baking. This will make it easier to lift in and out of the oven and prevent any spillage burning on the bottom of the oven.

- If traveling with the tart, put it back into the ring to make carrying easier and safer, and wrap in a clean dish towel.

making pastry dough

basic shortcrust pastry dough

This is the classic method for making short and crumbly shortcrust. It is made with half butter and half lard or vegetable shortening—the butter for color and flavor, and the shortening for shortness (crumble-factor). If you have cool hands, the hand method is best, because more air will be incorporated than if you use a food processor. If you have hot hands, the food processor is a blessing! The quantities of water added vary according to the humidity of the flour, so always add less than the recipe says—you can add more if the dough is dry, but once it is a sticky mess, your dough could be a disaster!

2 cups all-purpose flour

a pinch of salt

4½ tablespoons vegetable shortening or lard, chilled and diced

6 tablespoons unsalted butter, chilled and diced

2–3 tablespoons ice water

makes about 14 oz. dough, enough to line a 10-inch tart pan or to make a double crust for a deep 8-inch pie plate

Note The quantities given here are generous. Any leftover dough may be frozen or used to make small tartlets. It is not really worth making dough in small batches—I often make double quantities, freezing one for later.

1 Sift the flour and salt together into a bowl. (Or sift into a food processor.)

2 Using your fingertips, rub in the shortening and butter until the mixture resembles bread crumbs. (Or add to the food processor and blend for 30 seconds for the same result.)

3 Add the water, mixing lightly with a knife to bring the dough together. (Or add to the food processor, and pulse for 10 seconds until the dough forms large lumps. Add another tablespoon of water and repeat if necessary.)

4 Knead lightly on a floured work surface, then shape into a flattened ball, wrap in plastic wrap, and chill for at least 30 minutes before rolling out.

rich shortcrust pastry dough

This is a wonderfully light and crumbly crust. It is made the same way as Basic Shortcrust Pastry Dough (page 12) but is enriched with egg and made with butter only. It is best used for richer pies and tarts, or where the crust is more than just a carrier for the filling and the taste of the crust is important. It can be made in a food processor, following the method given for Dill and Nutmeg Dough (page 15), or the classic way, directly on the work surface. The food processor method is quicker and easier, and there is no sticky mess to clear up. But the classic method gives a slightly lighter result—and besides, there is something satisfying about making dough by hand.

2 cups all-purpose flour, plus extra for dusting

1/2 teaspoon salt

9 tablespoons unsalted butter, chilled and diced

2 large egg yolks

2 tablespoons ice water

makes about 14 oz. pastry dough, enough to line the base of a 10-inch tart pan or make a double crust for a deep, 8-inch pie plate

1 Sift the flour and salt together into a bowl, then rub in the butter.

Note For a Sweet Shortcrust Pastry Dough, sift 2 tablespoons confectioners' sugar with the flour and salt.

2 Mix the egg yolks with the 2 tablespoons ice water. Add to the flour, mixing lightly with a knife.

Note The dough must have some water in it or it will be too difficult to handle. If it is still too dry, add a little more water, sprinkling it over the flour mixture 1 tablespoon at a time.

3 Invert the mixture onto a lightly floured work surface.

4 Knead lightly with your hands until smooth.

5 Form the dough into a ball.

6 Flatten slightly, wrap in plastic wrap, and chill for at least 30 minutes before rolling out.

dill and nutmeg pastry dough (above)

2 cups all-purpose flour, plus extra for dusting

a pinch of salt

1 teaspoon freshly grated nutmeg

¼ cup chopped fresh dill

9 tablespoons butter, chilled and diced

1 large egg yolk

2–3 tablespoons ice water

Put the flour, salt, nutmeg, and dill into a food processor, add the butter, and blend until the mixture looks like fine bread crumbs. Mix the egg yolk with the ice water and add to the machine. Blend again until it begins to form a ball; add another tablespoon of water if it is too dry and blend again. Transfer to a floured work surface and knead lightly until smooth, then shape into a flattened ball. Wrap in plastic wrap and chill for 30 minutes before rolling out.

cheese shortcrust pastry dough

2 cups all-purpose flour, plus extra for dusting

1 teaspoon salt

3 tablespoons freshly grated Parmesan cheese

9 tablespoons unsalted butter, chilled and diced

2 large egg yolks

2–3 tablespoons ice water

Sift the flour and salt into a bowl. Stir in the Parmesan, then rub in the butter. Mix the egg yolks with 2 tablespoons ice water, then stir into the flour mixture to bind to a firm but malleable dough (add another tablespoon of water if it is too dry, and blend again). Knead lightly until smooth then shape into a flattened ball. Wrap in plastic wrap and chill for at least 30 minutes before rolling out.

american pie crust dough

This recipe for a classic American pie crust was given to me by a good friend from New York state. The quantity is enough for two pies—she makes and bakes one straight away and freezes the rest for another time. You could make and bake both pies now, freeze all the dough to use later, or make double quantity and freeze it all. To give the crust a richer flavor and delightful golden color, unsalted butter can be substituted for the vegetable shortening or you can use half butter and half vegetable shortening (or lard). It is a very light, crumbly crust when baked—similar to shortcrust and with a real homemade feeling.

$2^3/_4$ cups all-purpose flour. plus extra for dusting

a good pinch of salt

$1^1/_3$ cups vegetable shortening, chilled

1 large egg, beaten

1 tablespoon wine vinegar or lemon juice

$^1/_4$ cup ice water

makes about 1$^1/_2$ lb. pastry dough, enough for 2 single deep pie crusts, 9 inches diameter

1 Sift the flour and salt into a large bowl.

2 Cut in the shortening using 2 round-bladed knives or a pastry blender (or do this in a food processor).

3 Beat the egg in a separate bowl.

4 Stir the vinegar or lemon juice into the egg, then add the water.

5 Pour the wet mixture into the dry mixture, then cut it in with the knives or pastry blender again.

6 Bring the dough together quickly, using your hands.

7 Knead until smooth, either in the bowl or on a floured work surface.

Divide in 2 so it is easier to roll out later.

8 Shape the 2 balls of dough into flattened balls, wrap in plastic wrap, then chill for at least 30 minutes before rolling out.

Baking and freezing

Roll out each piece to about $1/8$ inch thick. Line both tart pans, prick all over with a fork, and chill or freeze for 15 minutes. Line with foil or parchment paper and fill with baking beans. For partial baking, bake at 400°F for 10–12 minutes, or, for full baking, 15–18 minutes until just coloring around the edges. Remove the foil or paper and beans (cool and reserve them for another day), then return the crusts to the oven to dry out for 4–5 minutes until golden.

For freezing, divide the uncooked dough in 2 and form into flattened balls ready to thaw and roll out.

rolling out, lining a tart pan, and baking blind

The secret of a beautiful crisp tart crust lies in these crucial initial stages of making the pie crust. The dough should be rolled out as thinly as you dare, lifted into the pan without being stretched, then gently eased in and trimmed. The uncooked crust must be chilled or frozen before baking to combat shrinkage. Baking blind will ensure that the tart does not have a soggy base. Keep the baked base in the pan while the filled tart is cooking or it could collapse.

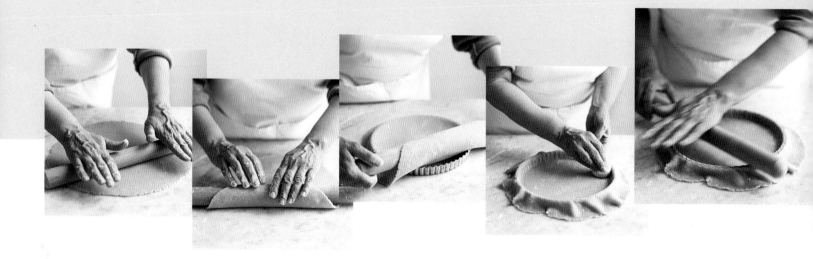

1 Preheat the oven to 400°F, or 375°F for doughs with a lot of sugar in them. Roll out the dough as thinly as necessary, about ⅛ inch thick, to line the dish you are using.

Note Ovens vary so you may need slightly lower settings than these. Oven temperatures for Pâte Sucrée and Puff Pastry also vary (see page 26 and page 29).

2 To line a tart pan, roll the flour-dusted dough around the rolling pin to help you pick it up—this will avoid stretching the dough, which might shrink during cooking.

3 Lower the dough over the pan and unroll to cover.

4 Use a small piece of extra dough wrapped in plastic wrap to help to push the dough into the edges of the pan. Once this is done you can press the dough up the sides of the pan.

5 Use the rolling pin to roll over the top—it will cut off any excess dough very neatly. Alternatively, cut off the overhang with a very sharp knife.

I also like to press the dough into the flutes of the ring after I've cut off the excess, to give a good shape.

6 Prick the base all over with a fork, then chill or freeze for 15 minutes to set the dough.

7 Line with foil or parchment paper (flicking the edges inwards towards the center so that they don't catch on the dough), then fill with baking beans.

Set on a baking sheet and bake blind in the center of the oven for 10–12 minutes.

8 Remove the foil or parchment paper and the baking beans, and return the pie crust to the oven for 5–7 minutes longer to dry out completely.

9 To prevent the crust from becoming soggy from an particularly liquid filling, brush the blind-baked crust with beaten egg—you can do this when it is hot or cold. Bake again for 5–10 minutes until set and shiny. This will also fill and seal any holes made when pricking before the blind baking.

10 If necessary, repeat the sealing process until an impervious layer has been built.

making small party tarts

Making your own little tarts takes less time than you think. They are very impressive, and are a good way of using up any leftover dough if a large tart doesn't use a full quantity. Shortcrust doughs give a homemade feel, but for true finesse, use Pâte Brisée (page 24) for savory tarts and Pâte Sucrée (page 26) for sweet ones. They can be frozen in the pan or cooked, cooled, and stored in an airtight container.

1 Preheat the oven to 400°F, or 375°F if the dough has a high sugar content. Roll out the dough thinly, to about 1/8 inch, on a floured work surface and use a plain or fluted dough cutter to stamp out small rounds slightly larger than the cups in your pan.

2 Carefully ease each dough round into the pan, avoiding stretching the dough. Press into the base using a small piece of dough wrapped in plastic wrap. Prick the base with a fork, then chill or freeze for 15 minutes.

3 Line each base with parchment paper or aluminum foil, then fill with baking beans. Bake blind for 5–10 minutes, depending on the size. Remove the foil or parchment paper and return to the oven for 1–2 minutes longer to dry out.

using phyllo pastry

Phyllo is a paper-thin, almost see-through dough from Greece. It is sold fresh or frozen in sheets rolled up in a package. Look for the authentic Greek phyllo rather than supermarket brands, which tend to be thicker and coarser.

The important thing to remember when using phyllo is not to let it dry out. Once it dries out, it cracks and is impossible to use. Always keep it in a plastic bag or under a slightly damp cloth or sheet of plastic wrap.

Cut all the dough into the appropriate size at once, and store in the plastic bag while you paint each sheet with melted butter to give it flavor and color. Some people use olive oil, but I find butter is best.

Use as soon as the dough is buttered, whether filling, rolling, folding, or pressing into a tart mold.

Phyllo is baked at 400°F to set it, then the oven is turned down to 375°F to finish and brown the pastry evenly. Don't cook it at a lower temperature or it will become soggy.

lattice tops

The lattice top gives a pretty decorative finish to a tart, teasingly half-concealing what lies beneath. There are many ways of doing this by hand—you can simply arrange the strips over each other, interweave them, or twist them to give a barley-sugar effect. If this looks too difficult and time-consuming, use a lattice cutter to create a lovely lacy effect. If there is no dough rim, set a ring of dough around the edge of the filled tart to keep the strips in place.

14 oz. pastry dough will line and lattice a 9-inch tart pan

Note You will need utensils such as a very sharp knife, a ruler or straight edge, or a lattice cutter (optional)

The classic method

1 Roll out the dough thinly. Decide how many strips will fit across the tart. Cut into equal strips with the knife, using the ruler or edge as a guide.

2 If there is no rim or it is not wide enough to support the lattice, cut out a ring of dough to fit inside the edge of the tart. Dampen the edge, then start arranging the strips at equal intervals across the filled tart. If you are not sure about where to position the strips, lay them halfway across at first, folding them back so that they can be easily moved if necessary.

3 Set a second set of strips across the first, either interweaving them like basketwork, or simply setting them at right angles across the first set of strips.

4 Trim the edges of the strips for a neat finish.

decorative edges

There are countless ways of decorating pastry edges on a tart—many designs are steeped in tradition and specifically used for particular tarts. The simplest is the forked edge, followed by using the tip of a knife to create cuts and folds. The edge is normally brushed with milk or beaten egg to give a soft sheen or shiny glaze.

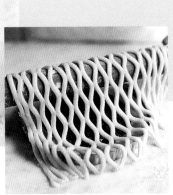

Using a lattice cutter

1 Roll out the dough to a size slightly larger than the tart. Roll the cutter the length of the dough, pressing firmly to make clean cuts.

2 Gently pull the lattice open and drape over a rolling pin. Lift carefully onto the tart, opening the mesh evenly. Press firmly around the edges to seal, trim off the excess, and finish with a decorative edge (see right).

Fork edge

The edge of the dough is marked by pressing the tines of the fork flat across the surface, so that the marks radiate outwards. Press quite hard to make deep indentations, then chill for 10 minutes to set.

Dog edge

These cuts look rather like a dog's floppy ears, hence the name! Using a sharp knife, make small cuts the width of the dough edge, about a thumb's breadth apart. Fold every alternate "ear" over towards the center of the pan and press the edge (not the fold) to seal. Chill for 10 minutes.

Devil edge

I call this design "devil edge" because I think it looks jaggedly devilish! It is the traditional edge for a treacle tart. Using a sharp knife, make small cuts the width of the dough edge about a thumb's breadth apart. Fold over every "flap" diagonally onto itself towards the center of the pan, pressing the tips (not the folds) downwards to seal. Chill for 10 minutes.

pâte brisée

This dough is really the French version of an unsweetened shortcrust. It has a finer texture so should be rolled out much thinner—to about ⅛ inch. Sometimes unsweetened pâte brisée is used for fruit tarts that are baked for a long time, because other pastries with a high sugar content would scorch before the fruit was cooked. This dough provides a firm, crisp support for the fruit. Don't be tempted to leave out the water in either this or the recipe for Pâte Sucrée (page 26)—it makes the dough stronger and easier to handle in the end.

1½ cups all-purpose flour, plus extra for dusting

a large pinch of salt

8 tablespoons (1 stick) unsalted butter, diced, at room temperature

1 large egg yolk

2½–3 tablespoons ice water

makes about 12 oz. pastry dough, enough to line a 10-inch tart pan or six 3-inch tartlet pans

The classic method

1 Sift the flour and salt into a mound on a clean work surface.

2 Make a well in the middle with your fist.

3 Put the butter and egg yolk into the well and, using the fingers of one hand, "peck" the eggs and butter together until they look like scrambled eggs.

4 Using a spatula or pastry scraper, flick the flour over the egg mixture and chop through until almost incorporated.

In the food processor

This method is useful if you are nervous about making dough or have very hot hands. (I have increased the ingredients here so the quantity will work well in a food processor.)

2 cups all-purpose flour

1 teaspoon salt

9 tablespoons unsalted butter, softened

1 extra-large egg yolk

2½–3 tablespoons ice water

makes about 14 oz.

5 Sprinkle with the water, and chop again.

6 Bring together quickly with your hands. Knead lightly into a ball, then flatten slightly.

7 Wrap in plastic wrap and chill for at least 30 minutes. Let it return to room temperature before rolling out.

1 Sift the flour and salt together onto a sheet of wax paper.

2 Put the butter and egg yolk into a food processor and blend until smooth, then add the water and blend again.

3 Add the flour and salt, and pulse until just mixed.

4 Transfer to a lightly floured work surface and knead gently until smooth. Form into a ball, flatten slightly and wrap in plastic wrap.

5 Chill in the refrigerator for at least 30 minutes. Let the dough return to room temperature before rolling out.

pâte sucrée

This is the classic French sweet pastry sometimes known as pâte sablée or "sandy pastry," because it has a fine crumbly texture when broken. Its high sugar content means that it can burn very easily—use a timer! It takes slightly longer to blind bake than other pastries—bake at the standard 375° for 15 minutes, then reduce the temperature to 350°F and cook for a further 10 minutes longer to dry out completely.

1½ cups all-purpose flour, plus extra for dusting

a pinch of salt

¼ cup sugar or confectioners' sugar

6 tablespoons unsalted butter, diced, at room temperature

2 large egg yolks

½ teaspoon vanilla extract

2–3 tablespoons ice water

makes about 14 oz. pastry dough, enough to line a tart pan, 10 inches diameter or 6 tartlet pans, 3 inches diameter

In the food processor

1 Sift the flour and salt onto a sheet of wax paper.

2 Put the sugar, butter, egg yolks, and vanilla extract into a food processor, then blend until smooth.

3 Add the water and blend again.

4 Add the flour to the food processor.

Pâte Sucrée can also be made by hand, as shown in the previous recipe Pâte Brisée on page 24.

5 Blend until just mixed.

6 Transfer to a lightly floured work surface. Knead gently until the dough is smooth.

7 Form into a flattened ball, then wrap in plastic wrap. Chill or freeze for at least 30 minutes.

Let return to room temperature before rolling out. This is quite a delicate dough to roll, so be sure to use enough (but not too much) flour when rolling.

1 Sift flour, salt, and sugar into a mound on a clean work surface.

2 Make a well in the middle with your fist.

3 Put the butter, egg yolks, and vanilla extract into the well. Using the fingers of one hand, "peck" the eggs and butter together until the mixture looks like creamy scrambled eggs.

4 Flick the flour over the egg mixture and chop it through with a spatula or pastry scraper, until it is almost incorporated but looking very lumpy.

5 Sprinkle with the water and chop again.

6 Bring together quickly with your hands. Knead lightly into a ball, then flatten slightly.

7 Wrap in plastic wrap, then chill for at least 30 minutes before using. Let return to room temperature before rolling.

puff pastry dough

This is the most difficult of all the layered pastries but, once mastered, it is relatively easy to do as long as you stick to the rules of resting and chilling. It is worth the effort—the flavor and texture means it is like biting into a buttery cloud! Flaky pastry involves dotting a dough with lard or shortening and butter before rolling and folding. It is a more complicated version of rough puff, which I prefer. Unless otherwise stated, puff pastry should be baked blind at 450°F, to enable it to rise quickly; then lower the oven to 400°F for the final drying-out stage.

2 cups all-purpose flour,
plus extra for dusting

¼ teaspoon salt

2 sticks plus 2 tablespoons
butter, in 1 piece at cool
room temperature*

1 teaspoon lemon juice

½–⅔ cup ice water

**makes about 1½ lb. pastry
dough, enough to line a
12-inch tart pan**

*The butter must be
malleable but not melting.*

1 Sift the flour and salt
into a large bowl.

2 Rub in one-quarter of
the butter with your hands.

3 Sprinkle with the lemon
juice and ½ cup of the
water.

4 Mix with the knife until
the dough starts to come
together in a lump. Add
the rest of the water,
1 tablespoon at a time,
if the mixture is dry.

(continued overleaf)

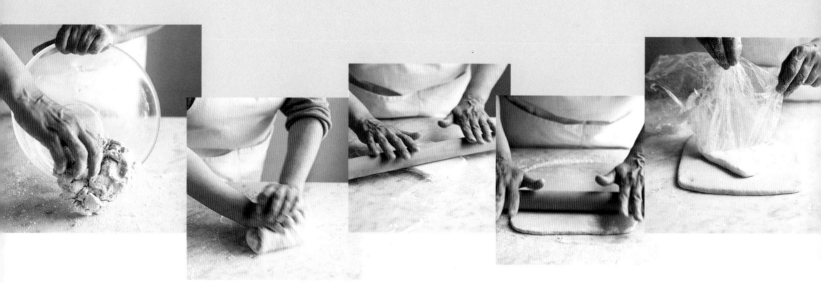

5 Transfer to a floured work surface.

6 Knead lightly to form a smooth ball. Flatten the ball with the palm of your hand, then wrap the dough in plastic wrap and chill for about 30 minutes until firm.

7 Put the remaining butter between sheets of parchment paper, then roll or beat with a rolling pin to make a square about ½ inch thick.

8 Unwrap the dough and roll out into a square large enough to wrap around the butter.

9 Put the butter in the center of the dough.

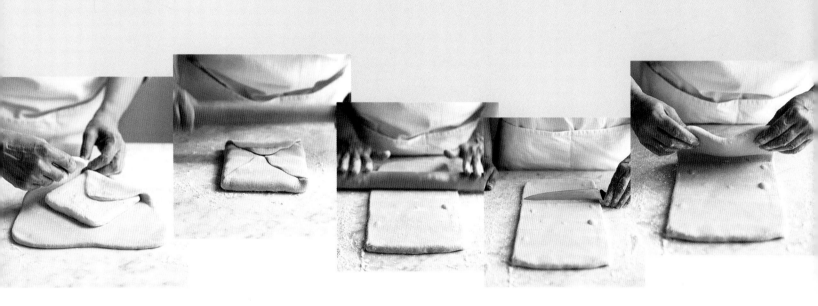

10 Bring the corners up and over to cover the butter completely.

11 Dust the rolling pin and both sides of the dough package with flour.

Take the rolling pin and make 3 or 4 impressions on the surface of the dough package to start the dough rolling.

12 Roll into a long rectangle three times longer than it is wide—you don't need exact measurements here but the dough should be about 1/2 inch thick.

Remove any excess flour using a dry pastry brush.

13 Lightly mark the rectangle into 3 equal sections, using the blunt edge of a knife.

14 Fold the third that is closest to you up over the middle third.

(continued overleaf)

15 Bring the top third towards you over the folded two-thirds. (This is the first roll and fold.)

16 Give the dough a quarter turn counter-clockwise so that it looks like a closed book, with the long open edge to the right. Make a finger mark in the dough to remind you that you have rolled and folded it once (next time, make 2 marks and so on). Rewrap and chill for 15 minutes.

17 Return the dough to the work surface in the closed-book position.

Seal the 3 edges lightly with a rolling pin to stop them from sliding out of shape.

18 Now roll out, away from you in one direction only, until the dough forms the same-size rectangle as before. Fold in the same way as before, wiping off any excess flour with the pastry brush.

Note It is important to be consistent about the direction of rolling and folding in order to build up the leaves of the pastry; always start with the long open edge to your right.

19 Make 2 indentations in the the dough (to indicate 2 roll-and-folds), then wrap and chill for 15 minutes. Do this rolling and folding 5 more times (a total of 7 rollings), then the dough is ready to use.

Chill for 30 minutes before rolling to its final shape, then chill again for at least 30 minutes.

20 When the dough has been cut to shape, the edges are gently tapped with the blade of a sharp knife to separate the layers and ensure a good rise.

rough puff pastry dough

This is a quick way to make good puff pastry. Needless to say, you must work very quickly, and it takes a little practice. Rolling and folding the dough creates layers of pastry and pockets of butter. The cooked pastry will be buttery, puffy, and light if made well; there is absolutely no comparison with bought puff pastry. Make a large quantity at one time and freeze what you don't use—it is easier to make in bulk and you will always have some on hand when you need it. A dash of lemon juice is sometimes added with the water to strengthen the layers of dough.

2 cups all-purpose flour, plus extra for dusting

a pinch of salt

12 tablespoons (1½ sticks) unsalted butter, chilled

½–⅔ cup ice water

makes about 1¼ lb. pastry dough, enough to line a 12-inch tart pan

1 Sift the flour and salt into a large bowl.

2 Quickly cut the butter into small cubes, about the size of the top of your little finger. Add to the flour mixture.

3 Stir the butter into the flour with a round-bladed knife so that it is evenly distributed.

4 Sprinkle the water over the surface, mixing in with knife as you do so.

(continued overleaf)

5 Mix with the knife until the dough starts to come together in a messy lump.

6 Transfer to a floured work surface. Knead lightly until it forms a streaky, rather lumpy ball. Flatten the ball with the palm of your hand, then wrap in plastic wrap the dough and chill for about 30 minutes until firm.

7 Unwrap and roll out away from you into a long rectangle that is three times longer than it is wide—no exact measurements are needed here, but it should be about ½ inch thick.

Remove any excess flour with a dry pastry brush.

8 Lightly mark the dough into 3 equal sections using a blunt knife.

9 Now fold the third closest to you up over the middle third.

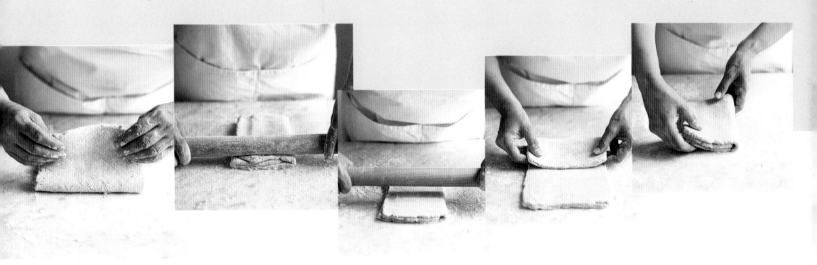

10 Bring the top third towards you over the folded two-thirds.

11 Give the dough a quarter turn counter-clockwise so that it looks like a closed book.

Seal the 3 edges lightly with a rolling pin to stop them sliding out of shape.

12 Now roll out, always away from you in one direction, until it is the same size rectangle as before.

13 Fold in the same way as before.

14 Make a finger indentation on the dough to indicate you that you have completed 1 roll and fold process, then wrap and chill for 15 minutes. Do this rolling and folding 4 more times (indenting it each time to indicate the number of roll-and-folds completed).

Chill for 30 minutes, then roll to its final shape. Chill again for at least 30 minutes.

cheat's rough puff pastry dough

A great friend showed me how to do this. It is very easy—but the butter must be very hard. It is made in exactly the same way as the Rough Puff Pastry Dough except that you freeze and grate the butter, then roll and fold the dough as quickly as you can. He swears that it is lighter made with margarine—I prefer using butter!

2 cups all-purpose flour, plus extra for dusting

a pinch of salt

12 tablespoons (1½ sticks) unsalted butter, frozen

about ½–⅔ cup ice water

makes about 1 lb. dough, enough to line a 12-inch tart pan with a false bottom

1 Sift the flour and salt into a large bowl.

2 Hold the butter in a dish towel and, using the large side of a box grater, quickly grate the butter into the flour.

3 Stir the butter into the flour with a round-bladed knife until evenly distributed.

4 Sprinkle the water over the surface, then mix with the knife until the dough starts to come together in a messy lump.

5 Transfer to a floured work surface and knead lightly until it forms a streaky, rather lumpy ball.

6 Flatten the ball with the palm of your hand. Wrap in plastic wrap and chill for 30 minutes until firm.

7 Unwrap and roll out away from you into a rectangle 3 times longer than it is wide—no exact measurements are needed here, but it should be about ½ inch thick.

8 Remove any excess flour with a pastry brush.

9 Lightly mark the dough into 3 equal sections with a blunt knife.

10 Fold the third closest to you up over the middle third, then bring the top third towards you over the folded two-thirds.

11 Make a finger mark in the dough to indicate you have completed 1 roll, then fold. Rewrap and chill for 15 minutes.

12 Repeat twice more (indenting each time with the number of roll-and-folds completed). Wrap and chill for 30 minutes.

13 Roll to the final shape, then chill for 30 minutes.

my just-push-it-in pastry dough or pâte frolle (almond pastry)

This sweet almond pastry dough is made in both France and Italy. Overworked, it is tough—but properly made, it is crisp and light. It is almost impossible to roll out, so I shape it into a sausage, then wrap in plastic wrap and chill until firm. I then slice it into thin rounds and push these into the base of the pan, pressing all over to make an even base.

1½ cups all-purpose flour

a pinch of salt

⅔ cup confectioners' sugar

2½ oz. ground almonds*

6 tablespoons unsalted butter, cubed, at room temperature

2 large egg yolks

½ teaspoon vanilla extract

2–3 tablespoons ice water

makes about 1 lb. pastry dough, enough to line a 9 to 10-inch tart pan

If ground almonds are unavailable in the baking section of your supermarket, grind blanched almonds in a blender, then measure out ⅔ cup. Store the remainder in an airtight container in the refrigerator.

The classic way

1 Sift flour, salt, and sugar into a mound on a clean work surface.

2 Sprinkle the ground almonds on top of the flour.

3 Make a well in the middle with your fist.

4 Put the butter, egg yolks, and vanilla extract into the well. Using the fingers of one hand, "peck" the eggs and butter together until the mixture resembles creamy scrambled eggs.

(continued overleaf)

5 Flick the flour over the egg mixture and chop it through with a spatula, until it is almost incorporated but still very lumpy.

6 Sprinkle with the water and chop again.

7 Bring together quickly with your hands and knead lightly, then shape into a thick sausage.

8 Wrap in plastic wrap and chill for at least 2 hours.

9 Unwrap and cut into thin slices.

In the food processor

This method makes the whole process much easier—and no sticky mess on the table to clean up afterwards. It keeps the dough cool, so is useful on a hot day, or if you have hot hands. As always, take care not to overwork the dough, because this can toughen it.

10 Push the slices into the base and sides of the pan, overlapping them very slightly and pushing together so that they form an even layer.

11 Chill or freeze for at least 30 minutes.

1 Sift the flour and salt onto a sheet of wax paper, then add the almonds.

2 Put the sugar, butter, egg yolks, and vanilla extract into a food processor and blend until smooth. Add the water and blend again.

3 Add the flour mixture and blend again until everything is just mixed.

4 Transfer to a lightly floured work surface and knead gently until smooth. Form into a long sausage, then wrap in plastic wrap. Chill in the refrigerator for at least 2 hours.

5 Cut into slices and push into the base and sides of the pan. Chill or freeze for 30 minutes.

savory tarts

quiche lorraine

A classic tart from Alsace and Lorraine, and the forerunner of many copies. Made well and with the best ingredients, this simplest of dishes is food fit for kings. I like to add a little grated Gruyère to the filling.

1 recipe Basic Shortcrust Pastry Dough (page 13) or Cheat's Rough Puff Pastry Dough, chilled (page 39)

8 oz. bacon, chopped, or cubed prosciutto

5 large eggs

¾ cup heavy cream or crème fraîche

freshly grated nutmeg, to taste

½ cup grated Gruyère cheese, about 2 oz.

sea salt and freshly ground black pepper

a tart pan, 9 inches diameter

serves 4–6

If using Basic Shortcrust Pastry Dough, bring to room temperature. Preheat the oven to 400°F.

Roll out the dough thinly on a lightly floured work surface and use to line the tart pan. Prick the base, chill or freeze for 15 minutes, then bake blind, following the method given on page 19.

Heat a nonstick skillet and sauté the bacon or prosciutto until brown and crisp, then drain on paper towels. Sprinkle over the base of the pie crust.

Put the eggs and cream or crème fraîche into a bowl, beat well, and season with salt, pepper, and nutmeg to taste. Carefully pour the mixture over the bacon and sprinkle with the Gruyère.

Bake for about 25 minutes until just set, golden brown, and puffy. Serve warm or at room temperature.

onion, rosemary, and roasted garlic tartlets

Toasting the whole garlic cloves in oil gives them a sweet nuttiness, and almost caramelizes them. They are blended into a custard with lots of rosemary, then cooked in the mini tartlet shells to make deliciously rustic appetizers. Serve with a big red wine to match the robust flavors.

½ recipe Rich Shortcrust Pastry Dough (page 14) or Pâte Brisée (page 24)

onion and garlic filling

6 tablespoons butter

1¼ lb. sweet onions, sliced

1 teaspoon salt

1¼ cups heavy cream or crème fraîche

2 sprigs of rosemary

6 large garlic cloves

olive oil

4 large egg yolks

freshly grated nutmeg, to taste

2 tablespoons chopped fresh rosemary

sea salt and freshly ground black pepper

30 Kalamata black olives, chopped, or rosemary sprigs, to finish

6 individual tartlet pans or 15 mini ones (you could use a mini-muffin pan)

makes 6 tartlets or 12–15 mini tartlets

Bring the dough to room temperature. Preheat the oven to 400°F.

Roll out the dough thinly on a lightly floured surface and use to line the tart pans, then prick the bases, chill or freeze for 15 minutes, and bake blind following the method on page 19.

Melt the butter in a large saucepan and add the onions, stirring to coat. Add a few tablespoons of water and the 1 teaspoon salt, and cover with a lid. Steam very gently for 30 minutes to 1 hour (trying not to look too often!) until meltingly soft. When the onions are cooked, remove the lid and cook for a few minutes to evaporate any excess liquid—the mixture should be quite thick. Let cool.

Put the cream or crème fraîche and rosemary leaves into a saucepan and heat until almost boiling. Remove from the heat and leave to infuse for as long as possible.

Put the garlic cloves into a small saucepan and just cover with olive oil. Simmer over gentle heat for 40 minutes or until the garlic is golden and soft.*

Remove the garlic from the oil (which you can keep to make salad dressings). Strain the cooled flavored cream into a blender and add the cooked garlic and egg yolks. Season to taste with salt, pepper, and nutmeg, and blend until smooth. Stir in the chopped rosemary.

Set the tartlet pie crusts on a baking sheet. Spoon the cooled onions evenly into the crusts, filling just half full. Pour the rosemary and garlic cream over the top. Bake for 15–20 minutes (depending on size) or until set and pale golden brown.

Serve warm, topped with chopped olives or a sprig of rosemary.

*****Note** To make a larger quantity of caramelized garlic cloves, wrap a whole unpeeled head of garlic in aluminum foil and roast at 375°F for about 45 minutes until soft. Open the foil and squeeze the garlic out of the skins.

flamiche

(a melting leek tart from Belgium)

½ recipe Rich Shortcrust Pastry Dough (page 14) or Pâte Brisée Dough (page 24)*

6 tablespoons butter

2 lb. leeks, split, well washed, and thickly sliced

1 teaspoon salt

4 large egg yolks

1¼ cups heavy cream or crème fraîche

freshly grated nutmeg, to taste

sea salt and freshly ground black pepper

a tart pan, 8 inches diameter

a baking sheet

serves 4–6

*Make the full amount and cook 2 crusts, freezing 1 for later use.

There is nothing quite like the combination of meltingly soft sweet leeks, cream, and pastry. This tart is perfect for a picnic served with some pâté and cold meats.

Bring the dough to room temperature. Preheat the oven to 400°F.

Roll out the dough thinly on a lightly floured work surface, then use to line the tart pan, prick the base, then chill or freeze for 15 minutes. Bake blind following the method on page 19.

Melt the butter in a large saucepan and add the leeks, stirring to coat. Add a few tablespoons of water and the 1 teaspoon salt, and cover with a lid. Steam very gently for at least 30 minutes (trying not to look too often!) until soft and melting. Remove the lid and cook for a few minutes to evaporate any excess liquid—the mixture should be quite thick. Let cool.

Put the egg yolks and cream or crème fraîche into a bowl, add salt, pepper, and nutmeg to taste, and beat well. Set the pie crust on a baking sheet. Spoon the cooled leeks evenly into the pie crust, fluffing them up a bit with a fork. Pour the egg mixture over the top.

Bake for 30 minutes or until set and pale golden brown. Serve warm.

roquefort tart

with walnut and toasted garlic dressing

Roquefort is a salty French blue cheese that's made with ewes' milk, but you could substitute any good-quality blue cheese. Walnuts are the perfect partner for blue cheese, especially when combined with the sweetly toasted slivers of garlic in this dressing.

1 recipe Pâte Brisée (page 24)

8 oz. cream cheese, such as Philadelphia (about 1 cup)

2/3 cup heavy cream or crème fraîche

3 large eggs, beaten

7 oz. Roquefort or other good blue cheese (a scant 1 cup)

freshly ground black pepper

freshly grated nutmeg, to taste

3 tablespoons chopped fresh chives

walnut and toasted garlic dressing

3 garlic cloves

2 tablespoons olive oil

3 oz. walnut halves (about 1 cup)

1 tablespoon walnut oil

3 tablespoons chopped fresh parsley

a false-bottom tart pan, 10 inches diameter

serves 6

Bring the dough to room temperature. Preheat the oven to 400°F.

Roll out the dough thinly on a lightly floured work surface, then use to line the tart pan. Prick the base, chill or freeze for 15 minutes, then bake blind following the method on page 19.

To make the filling, put the cream cheese into a bowl and beat until softened. Beat in the cream and the eggs. Crumble in the blue cheese and mix gently. Season with lots of black pepper and nutmeg. The cheese is salty, so you won't have to add extra salt. Stir in the chives, and set aside.

Let the pie crust cool slightly and lower the oven temperature to 375°F. Pour the filling into the crust and bake for 30–35 minutes or until puffed and golden brown.

Meanwhile, to make the walnut and garlic dressing, slice the garlic into the thinnest of slivers. Heat the olive oil in a skillet and add the garlic and walnuts. Stir-fry until the garlic is golden and the walnuts browned. Stir in the walnut oil and parsley.

Serve the tart warm or at room temperature with the warm walnut and garlic dressing.

goat cheese, leek, and walnut tart

This light, creamy open tart is easy to make because there is no need to line a pan or bake blind—simply roll out the dough and top like a pizza. Goat cheese and walnuts are a great partnership, especially combined with soft, earthy leeks.

½ recipe Puff Pastry Dough (page 29)* or 8 oz. frozen puff pastry, thawed

4 tablespoons butter

4 small leeks, trimmed, well washed, dried, and sliced

8 oz. goat cheese log with rind, sliced

sea salt and freshly ground black pepper

walnut paste

4 oz. walnut pieces (about 1¼ cups)

3 garlic cloves, crushed

⅓ cup walnut oil

3 tablespoons chopped fresh parsley

a dinner plate, 11 inches diameter

a baking sheet

serves 4–6

If using homemade Puff Pastry Dough, make the full recipe and freeze the remainder for later use.

Preheat the oven to 400°F. Roll out the dough thinly on a lightly floured work surface and cut out an 11-inch circle using the dinner plate as a template. Set on a baking sheet and chill or freeze for at least 15 minutes.

Melt the butter in a large saucepan and add the leeks, stirring to coat. Add a few tablespoons of water and a teaspoon of salt, and cover with a lid. Steam very gently for at least 20 minutes (trying not to look too often!) until almost soft. Remove the lid and cook for a few minutes to evaporate any excess liquid. Let cool.

To make the walnut paste, blend the walnuts and garlic in a food processor with 2 tablespoons water. Beat in the walnut oil and stir in the parsley. Spread this over the dough, avoiding the rim.

Spoon the leeks into the pie crust base and top with the slices of goat cheese. Sprinkle with any remaining walnut paste. Season with salt and freshly ground black pepper and sprinkle with olive oil. Bake for 20 minutes until the crust is golden and the cheese bubbling and brown.

Sprinkle with more parsley and serve immediately.

1 recipe Rich Shortcrust Pastry Dough (page 14) or Pâte Brisée (page 24)

slow-roasted tomatoes

12–15 large ripe cherry tomatoes

2 garlic cloves, finely chopped

1 tablespoon dried oregano

¼ cup olive oil

sea salt and freshly ground black pepper

herby cheese filling

3 oz. full-fat soft cheese with garlic and herbs, such as Boursin, (⅓ cup)

1 large egg, beaten

⅔ cup heavy cream

¼ cup chopped fresh mixed herbs, such as parsley, basil, or chives

3 oz. feta cheese

sea salt and freshly ground black pepper

tiny sprigs of thyme or cut chives, to serve

a plain cookie cutter, 2 inches diameter

2 mini-muffin pans, 12 cups each

makes 24 tartlets

Tiny tartlets are great to serve with cocktails. These look stunning and have a secret pocket of feta cheese lurking in the creamy, herby filling underneath the tomatoes. Make double quantity of the roasted tomatoes— they keep well in the refrigerator and are great in salads.

slow-roasted tomato and herb tartlets with feta

Bring the dough to room temperature. Preheat the oven to 400°F.

Roll out the dough as thinly as possible on a lightly floured work surface. Use the cookie cutter to stamp out 24 circles. Line the muffin cups with the dough circles, then prick the bases and chill or freeze for 15 minutes. Bake blind following the method on page 19, then remove from the pans and let cool.*

Turn the oven down to 325°F. Cut the tomatoes in half horizontally. Arrange cut side up on a baking sheet. Put the chopped garlic, oregano, olive oil, and lots of ground pepper into a bowl and mix well, then spoon or brush over the cut tomatoes. Bake slowly in the oven for 1½–2 hours, checking every now and then. They should be slightly shrunk and still a brilliant red color—if too dark, they will taste bitter.**

Put the soft cheese into a bowl, add the egg, cream, and chopped herbs, and beat until smooth. Season well. Cut the feta into 24 small cubes that will fit inside the pie crusts.

When ready to bake, set the crusts on a baking sheet, put a cube of feta into each one, and top with the garlic and herb mixture. Bake in the preheated oven for 15–20 minutes or until the filling is set. Top each with a tomato half, a sprinkle of the cooking juices, and a thyme sprig or chive stem. Serve warm.

****Note** The pie crusts will keep for up to 1 week in an airtight container, but reheat to crisp them up before filling.

**Note Use the tomatoes right away or pack into a storage jar and cover with olive oil.

potato and parmesan tart with chives

Real comfort food for a miserable wet weekend! This is a deliciously creamy tart, which makes an unusual supper dish served with smoked salmon or a crunchy Caesar salad.

1 recipe Rich Shortcrust Pastry Dough (page 14)

2 lb. new or white potatoes, thinly sliced*

4 tablespoons butter, cubed

1/4 cup freshly chopped chives

freshly grated nutmeg, to taste

4 oz. freshly grated Parmesan cheese (about 1 1/4 cups)

1 large egg, beaten

1 1/4 cups heavy cream

sea salt and freshly ground black pepper

a deep, springform tart pan, 8 inches diameter, or any suitable dish with a 1-quart capacity

serves 4–6

Do not rinse the potatoes—their starch will help to thicken the cream.

Bring the dough to room temperature. Preheat the oven to 400°F.

Roll out the dough thinly on a lightly floured work surface. Use the dough to line the pan or dish (this can be a little tricky, so be patient and take your time), then prick the base. Chill or freeze for 15 minutes, then bake blind following the method on page 19.

After baking blind, turn down the oven to 325°F. Reserve 1/4 cup of the Parmesan. Layer the sliced potatoes and butter in the baked crust, sprinkling each layer with some of the remaining 1 cup Parmesan, chives, nutmeg, salt and pepper.

Layer the sliced potatoes and butter in the baked pie crust, seasoning the layers with the chives, salt, pepper, nutmeg, and 1 cup of the Parmesan.

Put the egg and cream into a bowl, beat well, then pour over the potatoes. Sprinkle the remaining Parmesan over the top. Bake for about 1 hour (it may take up to 15 minutes longer, depending on the type of potato used), or until the potatoes are tender and the top is dark golden brown.

Let cool for 10 minutes, then remove from the pan or dish. Alternatively, serve straight from the dish.

Note You could speed up the cooking time by precooking the filling in the microwave, but it will not look quite as good. Mix the sliced potatoes, pieces of butter, 1 cup of the Parmesan, nutmeg, half the cream, salt, and pepper in a non-metallic bowl. Cover, leaving a small hole for steam to escape, and microwave for 10 minutes on HIGH. Mix in the remaining cream and egg. Carefully spoon the mixture into the pie crust, sprinkling with chives as you go. Finish with the remaining Parmesan cheese and bake for about 30 minutes until tender.

A wickedly creamy tart that puffs up during baking, and is filled with the spring flavors of fresh asparagus and waxy new potatoes encased in a crisp nutmeg and dill pie crust.

chunky new potato and asparagus tart

1 recipe Dill and Nutmeg Pastry Dough (page 15)

1 lb. small new potatoes (or other waxy potatoes)

1 lb. fresh asparagus

4 whole large eggs, plus 2 yolks, beaten

2/3 cup sour cream or crème fraîche

sea salt and freshly ground black pepper

a little olive oil, to serve

a rectangular false-bottom tart pan, 8 x 12 inches

a baking sheet

serves 6–8

Bring the dough to room temperature. Preheat the oven to 400°F.

Roll out the dough thinly on a lightly floured work surface, then use to line the tart pan. Prick the base, chill or freeze for 15 minutes, then bake blind following the method given on page 19.

Turn the oven temperature down to 375°F. Meanwhile, boil the potatoes in salted water for 20 minutes until tender. While boiling, trim the asparagus and cut into 2-inch lengths. Reserve the tips. Add the asparagus stems to the potatoes 6 minutes before the potatoes are done.

Drain the vegetables and refresh in cold water, then thickly slice the potatoes. Put the eggs and sour cream or crème fraîche into a bowl, beat well, then season with salt and pepper.

Arrange the potatoes and asparagus over the base of the pie crust and pour in the egg mixture. Set on a baking sheet and bake for 25–30 minutes until puffed up and golden brown.

Meanwhile, cook the reserved asparagus tips in boiling salted water until tender, then drain and refresh. Toss the tips in a little olive oil and serve a spoonful with each portion. Serve warm.

creamy eggplant tart with slow-roasted cherry tomatoes

paprika and gruyère pastry dough

6 tablespoons butter

1 cup plus 2 tablespoons all-purpose flour, plus extra for dusting

1/2 teaspoon sweet paprika

1/2 teaspoon dry mustard powder

1/2 cup freshly grated Gruyère cheese

1 large egg yolk

2 tablespoons ice water

sea salt and freshly ground black pepper

slow-roasted tomatoes

1 lb. large ripe cherry tomatoes

2 garlic cloves, finely chopped

1 tablespoon dried oregano

1/4 cup olive oil

sea salt and freshly ground black pepper

eggplant filling

2 medium eggplants

2 garlic cloves, crushed

1/2 teaspoon sweet paprika

1 tablespoon dried oregano

3 large eggs, beaten

sea salt and freshly ground black pepper

2–3 tablespoons olive oil, to finish

a baking sheet

a rectangular tart pan, 10 x 6 inches

serves 6

The combination of creamy eggplant, garlic, and tomatoes sings of the sun. This is the perfect tart to eat on a hot summer's day, accompanied by a bitter leafy salad and a lot of warm chatter.

To prepare the tomatoes, preheat the oven to 325°F. Cut the tomatoes in half horizontally and arrange them cut side up on a baking sheet.

Put the garlic, oregano, olive oil, salt, and pepper into a bowl and mix well. Spoon or brush over the cut tomatoes. Bake slowly for about 2 hours, checking every now and then. They should be slightly shrunk and still a brilliant red color—if too dark, they will taste bitter. (You can use the tomatoes right away or pack into a container and cover with olive oil.)

To make the pastry dough, rub the butter into the flour until it resembles fine bread crumbs. Stir in the paprika, mustard, Gruyère, salt, and pepper. Mix the egg with 2 tablespoons cold water and mix into the flour for a soft dough. (Sprinkle with a little more water if the mixture is too dry.)

Knead until smooth, wrap in plastic wrap, and chill for 30 minutes. Use to line the tart pan, then prick the base and chill or freeze for 15 minutes. Preheat the oven to 400°F and bake blind following the method on page 19.

To make the filling, prick the eggplants all over and bake for 45 minutes or until soft. Remove from the oven and let cool. (Or prick each eggplant in 2–3 places and microwave on HIGH for about 12 minutes until soft.)

Turn down the oven to 350°F. Halve the eggplants and scoop out the flesh into a food processor. Add the garlic, paprika, oregano, eggs, salt, and pepper to taste, then blend until smooth. Pour into the pie crust and bake for about 25 minutes or until set.

Remove from the oven and let cool. Arrange the roasted tomatoes over the surface to cover completely. Sprinkle with the olive oil (or use oil from the jar if you have stored the tomatoes), then serve.

These are completely vegetarian, and completely delicious! To get a really smoky grilled flavor into the eggplants, try broiling or grilling them whole. You will have to turn them often to cook them evenly—make sure they are very charred and completely soft before using.

eggplant, mushroom, and cilantro tartlets

1 recipe Basic Shortcrust Pastry Dough (page 13)

eggplant, mushroom, and cilantro filling

2 medium eggplants

3 tablespoons olive oil

2 shallots, finely chopped

2 tablespoons crushed coriander seeds

1 lb. portobello mushrooms, finely chopped

3–4 tablespoons white wine

1 large egg, beaten

1/3 cup heavy cream

1 1/2 cups chopped cilantro

sea salt and freshly ground black pepper

8 small tartlet pans, 4 inches diameter

a baking sheet

makes 8 tartlets

Bring the dough to room temperature. Preheat the oven to 400°F. Roll the dough as thinly as you dare on a lightly floured work surface, then use to line the tartlet pans. Prick the bases, chill or freeze for 15 minutes, then bake blind following the method given on page 19.

Put the whole eggplants onto a baking sheet and bake for about 45 minutes or until soft and beginning to char.*

Meanwhile, heat the oil in a medium saucepan and add the shallots and coriander seeds. Cook gently for 5 minutes until the shallots are soft and golden. Stir in the mushrooms and wine and cook over high heat for 10 minutes or until all the liquid has evaporated.

Remove the eggplants from the oven. Split them open and scoop out the flesh. Chop the flesh coarsely and beat into the mushroom mixture. Beat in the egg and cream. Stir in the chopped cilantro and season well with salt and pepper. Cool, then chill before serving.

*Note Alternatively, you can cook a whole eggplant in the microwave by piercing it few times, wrapping in paper towels, and cooking on HIGH for 10–12 minutes. It won't have that smoky flavor, but will be very pale and creamy inside.

portobello mushroom and tarragon tart

1 recipe Cheese Shortcrust Pastry Dough (page 15)

6 tablespoons unsalted butter

1 onion, sliced

1 lb. portobello mushrooms, sliced

freshly squeezed juice of 1 lemon

2 tablespoons chopped fresh tarragon

8 oz. mascarpone cheese, softened (about 1 cup

3 extra-large eggs, beaten

sea salt and freshly ground black pepper

garlic crunch topping

4 tablespoons butter

1 cup dry bread crumbs

3 garlic cloves, chopped

finely grated zest of 1 unwaxed lemon

3 tablespoons chopped fresh parsley

a deep fluted tart pan, 10 inches diameter

serves 6–8

Portobello mushrooms are full of flavor—the darker, the better. This tart has a creamy filling laced with tarragon and lemon. The garlicky crunchy topping turns it into a giant version of a stuffed mushroom—but more sophisticated! Serve with a fresh tomato salad.

Bring the dough to room temperature. Preheat the oven to 400°F.

Roll out the dough thinly on a lightly floured work surface. Use to line the tart pan, then chill or freeze for 15 minutes and bake blind following the method given on page 19.

Melt the butter in a skillet, add the onion, and sauté until soft and golden. Add the mushrooms, lemon juice, salt, and pepper, then sauté over medium heat for 5 minutes until the mushrooms are tender and the liquid has evaporated. Stir in the tarragon, then let the mixture cool slightly.

To make the topping, melt the butter in a skillet, add the bread crumbs, garlic, lemon zest, and parsley, and sauté over high heat until the bread crumbs begin to crisp but not color too much. Tip the mixture into a bowl.

Put the mascarpone and eggs into a bowl and beat well. Stir in the mushroom mixture. Pour into the pie crust, then sprinkle with the topping and bake for 20–25 minutes until set, crisp, and golden on top. Serve warm.

pissaladière

(Provençal tomato and onion pizza)

yeast pastry dough

½ cake compressed yeast*

a pinch of sugar

1⅓ cups all-purpose flour,
plus extra for dusting

4 tablespoons chilled butter, cubed

1 large egg, beaten

a pinch of salt

olive oil, for the bowl

herby onion filling

3 tablespoons olive oil

3 lb. mild onions, thinly sliced

3 garlic cloves, chopped

2 teaspoons dried herbes de Provence

tomato sauce

1¾ lb. canned chopped tomatoes

3 tablespoons tomato purée

2 tablespoons olive oil

1 teaspoon harissa (chile-spice paste)

⅔ cup white wine

sea salt and freshly ground black pepper

to finish

15 anchovy fillets in oil,
halved lengthwise

olive oil, for sprinkling

18 very good black olives

a jelly roll pan, 15 x 10 inches

serves 6

**To use active dry yeast, mix
1 teaspoon with the flour, rub in the
butter, then continue as the main recipe.*

This Provençal version of Italian pizza is seen in every *boulangerie* in the south of France. There are many variations, and I've distilled them here into one perfect picnic food. Use any good olives, but I like the oven-dried Greek-style ones.

To make the onion filling, heat the oil in a large saucepan, add the onions, garlic, and 3 tablespoons water. Cover and cook over gentle heat for 1 hour or until meltingly soft, but not colored.** Stir the onions occasionally, making sure they don't burn. Stir in the herbs, then set a strainer over a bowl and tip the onions into the strainer. Reserve the caught juices for the yeast dough.

To make the dough, cream the fresh yeast and sugar in a bowl, then beat in 3 tablespoons of the reserved onion liquid. Leave for 10 minutes until frothy.

Sift the flour into a bowl and rub in the butter. Make a well in the center and add the egg, yeast mixture, and salt. Mix until it starts to come together, then transfer to a floured work surface and knead until smooth. Oil the bowl. Return the dough to the oiled bowl and put the bowl inside a large plastic bag. Let rise for about 1 hour or until doubled in size.

To make the tomato sauce, put all the ingredients into a saucepan, mix well, and bring to a boil. Simmer uncovered for about 1 hour, stirring occasionally until well reduced and very thick. Season well and set aside.

Preheat the oven to 375°F. Punch down the dough, knead, then roll out onto a lightly floured surface. Use to line the jelly roll pan, bringing the dough well up the edges.

Spread the tomato sauce over the base and cover with the onions. Arrange the anchovy fillets in a lattice over the onions. Sprinkle with olive oil, and bake for 1 hour until the crust is golden and crisp.

Dot with the olives and serve warm or at room temperature.

****Note** You can cook the onions quickly in a microwave. Toss the onions in the olive oil and put them into a non-metallic bowl. Cover, leaving a small gap for the steam to escape, then microwave on HIGH for 10 minutes. Continue as for the conventional method.

spicy crab in phyllo cups

9 small sheets phyllo pastry dough

4 tablespoons butter, melted

spicy crab filling

8 oz. canned white crab meat
in brine, drained

3 oz. canned water chestnuts, drained
and finely chopped or sliced

1 inch fresh ginger, peeled and
cut into fine strips

2 scallions, trimmed
and thinly sliced

finely grated zest and juice
of 1 unwaxed lime

1 garlic clove, crushed

½ fresh red chile, seeded and
finely chopped

2 teaspoons sesame oil

2 tablespoons chopped fresh cilantro

sea salt and freshly ground black pepper

*3 mini-muffin pans, 12 cups each,
brushed with melted butter*

makes about 36

These delicate bites are as light as air, but packed with fresh Asian flavors. I tend to use canned white crab meat from the Pacific for these—not only does it taste very good, but there is no shell or messy bits to deal with if you're catering for a large number of people. It is also much cheaper than fresh.

Preheat the oven to 350°F.

Unroll the phyllo and cut the stack into 108 pieces, 3 inches square. To do this, keep the sheets stacked on top of each other, then mark the top sheet into 12 squares. Cut down through all the layers, giving 108 squares. Pile into 2–3 stacks and keep beside you in a plastic bag.

To make a phyllo cup, take 3 squares of phyllo, brush each with melted butter, and set one on top of the other, so that the points make a star, and do not touch each other. Quickly but gently press into one of the cups of the prepared muffin pan, so the points of the phyllo shoot upwards like a handkerchief. Repeat with all the remaining phyllo until you have 36 cups.

Bake in the oven for 8–10 minutes until golden. Remove, let cool in the pan, then carefully remove to a tray (they are very fragile).

Put the crab into a bowl and fluff up with a fork. Stir in the water chestnuts, ginger, and scallions. In a separate bowl, mix the lime zest and juice, crushed garlic, chile, and sesame oil, and season to taste. Mix this into the crab mixture (this can be done up to 4 hours in advance), then stir in the cilantro.

Fill the cups with the crab mixture just before serving (they can go a little soggy if they are kept too long).

crab and sweet pickled chile tart

The sweet and salty taste of fresh crab (if you can get it) mixed with mild red chiles pickled in sweet vinegar is fantastic. They seem made for each other. Serve this with an avocado salsa or just plain sliced avocado dressed with a cilantro vinaigrette.

1 recipe Cheese Shortcrust Pastry Dough (page 15)

chile crab filling

2 tablespoons olive oil

a bunch of scallions, sliced

6 large eggs

1¼ cups heavy cream

1 tablespoon Dijon mustard

1 lb. fresh or frozen crab meat, thawed and drained

8 mild, sweet pickled red chile peppers, seeded and coarsely chopped

3 oz. freshly grated Parmesan (1 cup)

freshly ground black pepper

a deep false-bottom tart pan, 10 inches diameter

a baking sheet

serves 6–8

Bring the dough to room temperature. Preheat the oven to 400°F.

Put the dough onto a lightly floured work surface, roll out to a thickness of ⅛ inch and use to line the tart pan. Chill or freeze for 15 minutes, then bake blind following the method given on page 19. Let cool.

Reduce the oven temperature to 350°F. Heat the olive oil in a saucepan, add the scallions, and sauté until softened but not colored. Let cool slightly.

Put the eggs, cream, and mustard into a bowl and beat well. Stir in the crab, cooked scallions, sweet chile peppers, and Parmesan, then season with plenty of black pepper. Spoon into the pie crust and level the surface.

Set on a baking sheet and bake for about 45 minutes until just firm. Serve warm or at room temperature.

salmon, dill, and parmesan tart with pickled cucumber

1 recipe Rich Shortcrust Pastry Dough (page 14) or Pâte Brisée (page 24)

salmon and dill filling

1 lb. fresh salmon fillets (with or without skin)

1¼ cups heavy cream

3 oz. smoked salmon pieces (scraps will do, but cut off any brown bits)

3 large eggs, beaten

3 tablespoons chopped fresh dill

1 oz. freshly grated Parmesan cheese (⅓ cup)

sea salt and freshly ground black pepper

cucumber topping

2 large cucumbers

1 tablespoon sea salt

1 tablespoon sugar

½ cup white wine or cider vinegar

2 tablespoons chopped fresh dill

freshly ground white pepper

extra dill sprigs, to serve

a tart pan, 10 inches diameter

a baking sheet

serves 6–8

I make this tart extra special by blending in a little smoked salmon (you could also use gravlax) at the same time as the eggs and cream. This gives the tart a mysterious, slightly smoky flavor and a velvety texture.

Bring the dough to room temperature. Preheat the oven to 400°F.

Roll out the dough thinly on a lightly floured work surface, then use to line the tart pan. Chill or freeze for 15 minutes, then bake blind following the method given on page 19. Remove from the oven and turn the oven down to 375°F.

Put the salmon fillets into a shallow saucepan and cover with cold water. Add a little salt and bring slowly to a boil. Just before the water boils, turn off the heat and leave the salmon in the water until it is cold—by then it will be cooked and very moist. Lift it out of the water and drain well. Peel off any skin and check for any bones. Flake coarsely.

Put the cream into a blender, add the smoked salmon and eggs, then blend until smooth. Season with salt and pepper and stir in the dill. Sprinkle the salmon flakes over the base of the tart and pour in the smoked salmon and cream mixture. Sprinkle with the Parmesan, set on a baking sheet, and bake for 25 minutes, until just set. Remove from the oven and let cool completely.

Meanwhile, to make the cucumber topping, peel the cucumber, then slice as thinly as possible using a mandoline or a food processor. Spread in a colander and sprinkle with the salt, mixing well. Stand the colander on a plate and leave to drain for 30 minutes. Rinse well and squeeze the excess moisture out of the cucumber. Spread the cucumber over a large plate.

Dissolve the sugar in the vinegar and stir in the dill. Pour this over the cucumber and let marinate for at least 1 hour before serving.

To serve, drain the cucumber well and arrange it casually over the top of the salmon tart. Top with lots of white pepper and the dill sprigs, then serve immediately. Any extra salad can be served on the side.

smoked salmon, vodka, and sour cream aspic tartlets

½ recipe Rich Shortcrust Pastry Dough
(page 14) or ½ recipe Pâte Brisée
(page 24)*

flavored aspic

1 sheet of leaf gelatin**

⅔ cup light fish stock

1–2 tablespoons lemon-flavored vodka

2 tablespoons chopped fresh chives

smoked salmon filling

¼ cup sour cream

3 oz. smoked salmon, chopped
(or avruga or keta caviar)

whole chives, to finish

a 2-inch plain cookie cutter

2 mini-muffin pans, 12 cups each

makes 24 tartlets

*Make up the full amount and freeze the
rest for later use.*

Make these pretty little tartlets for a special occasion—they simply explode with fabulous flavors. I usually make these with smoked salmon, but use avruga (herring roe prepared like caviar) if you can find it—its almost smoky taste is just perfect with the hidden sour cream and chives.

Bring the dough to room temperature. Preheat the oven to 400°F.

Roll out the dough as thinly as possible on a lightly floured work surface, then stamp out 24 circles with the cookie cutter. Use these to line the cups of the mini muffin pans. Prick the bases and chill or freeze for 15 minutes. Bake blind using the method given on page 19, remove from the pans, and cool.***

To make the flavored aspic, soak the leaf gelatin in cold water for 2–3 minutes until soft. Warm the fish stock, then stir in the drained gelatin until dissolved. Add the vodka. Let cool until syrupy but still pourable, then stir in the chives.

Arrange the pie crusts on a tray and add ½ teaspoon sour cream to each tartlet. Cover with a mound of smoked salmon (or a little avruga or keta caviar), then spoon in enough aspic to fill to the top of the crust. Put in the refrigerator for 15–20 minutes to set, then garnish each one with a couple of thin chive stems. Serve immediately.

Note Leaf gelatin is best here, because it is flavorless. Powdered gelatin has a more defined taste, which can spoil the flavor of the fish. But if you do want to use it, use 1 level teaspoon. Take 3 tablespoons out of the stock and put it into a small bowl or teacup. Sprinkle the gelatin over the liquid, let it swell for 10 minutes, then heat gently to dissolve the gelatin. Stir into the remaining stock and use as above.

***Note** You can keep the bases in an airtight container for up to 1 week, but reheat to crisp them up before filling.

There is a fabulous blend of flavors in the filling. The mascarpone is dotted onto the sausage mixture before the onions are piled on top—so it just melts in.

sausage, sun-dried tomato, and potato tart

with golden onions

1 recipe Pâte Brisée (page 24)

sausage and onion filling

3 tablespoons olive oil

3 onions, thinly sliced

2 garlic cloves, finely chopped

8 oz. potatoes, chopped

12 oz. best-quality fresh pork sausages, skinned

1 tablespoon all-purpose flour

2–3 tablespoons tomato purée

12 sun-dried tomato halves in oil, chopped

1 teaspoon hot red pepper flakes

2 teaspoons dried herbes de Provence

6 oz. mascarpone cheese (⅔ cup)

sea salt and freshly ground black pepper

*a deep tart pan,
9 inches diameter, 1½ inches deep*

serves 4–6

Bring the dough to room temperature. Preheat the oven to 400°F.

Roll out the dough on a lightly floured work surface, then use to line the tart pan. Prick the base, then chill or freeze for 15 minutes. Bake blind following the method given on page 19.

To make the filling, heat the oil in a large saucepan, add the onions, garlic, and 3 tablespoons water. Cover and cook over gentle heat for about 1 hour or until meltingly soft but not colored. Stir the onions occasionally, making sure they don't stick.* Let cool.

Blanch the potatoes in boiling salted water for 1 minute, then drain and set aside. Heat a nonstick skillet and add the sausage meat, breaking it up with a fork or wooden spoon as it cooks and browns.

After about 5 minutes, stir in the flour, tomato purée, sun-dried tomatoes, hot red pepper flakes, herbs, and salt and pepper to taste. Cook for another 5 minutes, then stir in the potatoes. Spoon this into the pie crust and dot small spoonfuls of the mascarpone over the surface. Cover with a layer of the cooked onions, then bake for 25 minutes until the onions are golden.

*****Note** You can cook the onions quickly in a microwave. Toss them in the olive oil and put into a non-metallic bowl. Cover, leaving a small gap for the steam to escape, then microwave on HIGH for 10 minutes. Continue as for the conventional method.

sweet tarts

This is a tart filled with an uncooked lemon curd and baked in the oven until just firm. This recipe comes from my sister Jacks, who has a reputation for her fantastic lemon tarts. She has made very tiny ones for champagne receptions and weddings—if you are making bite-size morsels, the crusts must be wonderfully thin so that they melt in the mouth.

classic lemon tart

1 recipe Sweet Rich Shortcrust Pastry Dough (page 14, see note)

1 egg, beaten, to seal the dough

sour cream or crème fraîche, to serve (optional)

lemon filling

6 extra large eggs

2⅓ cups sugar

finely grated zest and strained juice of 4 juicy unwaxed lemons

1¼ sticks unsalted butter, melted

a false-bottom fluted tart pan, 9 inches diameter

a baking sheet

foil or parchment paper and baking beans

serves 8

Bring the dough to room temperature. Preheat the oven to 375°F.

Roll out the dough thinly on a lightly floured work surface, and use to line the tart pan. Chill or freeze for 15 minutes, then bake blind following the method given on page 19. Brush with beaten egg, then bake again for 5–10 minutes until set and shiny to prevent the filling from making the crust soggy.

Turn the oven down to 300°F. To make the lemon filling, put the eggs, sugar, lemon zest and juice, and butter into a food processor and blend until smooth.

Set the baked pie crust on a baking sheet and pour in the filling. Bake in the oven for about 1 hour (it may need a little longer, depending on your oven), until just set. Remove from the oven and let cool completely before serving.

Serve at room temperature, maybe with a spoonful of sour cream or crème fraîche, if using.

Note For a special occasion you can decorate this tart with candied shreds of lemon zest. Peel the zest only from 3 or 4 lemons, leaving behind any white pith. Cut the zest into very fine shreds with a very sharp knife. Make a sugar syrup by boiling 6 tablespoons sugar with ⅔ cup water. Stir in the shreds and simmer for about 10 minutes until tender and almost transparent. Carefully lift out of the syrup, drain, and sprinkle around the edge of the tart while still warm, to form a ring. Cool before serving.

I have been making this tart since I started cooking, at the tender age of eight—it used to be my *pièce de résistance*! Blending the sugar with large peelings of lemon zest transfers all the essential oils to the sugar and gives a wonderful aroma to the tart. Using cottage cheese instead of cream cheese gives a lighter texture and will cut the calories.

simple lemon cheese tart

1 recipe Sweet Rich Shortcrust Pastry Dough (page 14, see note)

1 unwaxed lemon

1/3 cup sugar

12 oz. cream cheese, such as Philadelphia (1 1/2 cups)

1 large egg, plus 3 egg yolks

2 teaspoons vanilla extract

a false-bottom tart pan, 9 inches diameter

foil or parchment paper and baking beans

serves 4–6

Bring the dough to room temperature. Preheat the oven to 375°F.

Roll out the dough on a lightly floured work surface and use to line the tart pan. Prick the base, then chill or freeze for 15 minutes. Bake blind following the method given on page 19. Let cool.

Peel the zest from the lemon leaving behind any white pith, and squeeze the juice. Put the zest and sugar into a food processor or small blender, and blend until the sugar and zest mixture looks damp.

Add the lemon juice and blend again—the lemon zest should be completely dissolved into the sugar. Add the cheese, egg yolks, whole egg, and vanilla extract. Blend until smooth and pour into the baked crust.

Bake for about 25 minutes until just set and lightly browned on top. Remove from the oven and let cool. Serve at room temperature.

This unusual almond and chocolate cookie crust is the perfect foil for a sharp lemon and almond filling.

lemon and almond tart with chocolate amaretti crust

8 oz. amaretti cookies or Italian ratafias

2 oz. bittersweet chocolate, grated or chopped

6 tablespoons butter, melted

lemon almond filling

3 unwaxed lemons

4 extra-large eggs

$1/2$ cup plus 2 tablespoons sugar

1 stick plus 2 tablespoons unsalted butter, melted

4 oz. ground almonds (1 cup plus 2 tablespoons)

$2/3$ cup sour cream or crème fraîche

a deep tart pan, 9 inches diameter, 1 inch deep

a baking sheet

serves 6–8

*If ground almonds are unavailable in the baking section of your supermarket, grind blanched almonds in a blender, then measure out 1 cup plus 2 tablespoons. Store the remainder in an airtight container in the refrigerator.

Preheat the oven to 350°F.

Put the amaretti cookies or ratafias into a food processor and blend until finely crushed. Add the chocolate and blend again. Pour in the melted butter and blend until well mixed and coming together.

Put the tart pan onto a baking sheet. Press the mixture evenly over the base and sides of the tart pan (a potato masher and the back of a small spoon will help here). Bake for 10 minutes to set the base. Remove from the oven and press the puffed-up crust down again.

Finely grate the zest from the lemons and squeeze and strain the juice. Beat the eggs in a bowl, then beat in the lemon zest and juice, sugar, melted butter, and ground almonds. Pour into the amaretti crust and bake for 25 minutes until set and very lightly brown on top.

Cool, then spread with the sour cream or crème fraîche and serve at room temperature.

In these delicious little tarts, a zesty lemon meringue puffs up like a cloud over a sea of blueberries, then sets to a featherlight cooked mousse. Irresistible!

blueberry and lemon cloud tartlets

1 recipe Pâte Brisée Dough (page 24)

lemon filling

4 extra-large eggs, separated

¾ cup sugar

finely grated zest of 2 unwaxed lemons or 3 limes

freshly squeezed juice of 1 lemon or 2 limes

a pinch of salt

1 lb. fresh blueberries (3 cups), plus extra to serve

confectioners' sugar, for dusting

sour cream or crème fraîche, to serve

8 tartlet pans, 4 inches diameter

a baking sheet

foil or parchment paper and baking beans

makes 8 tartlets

Bring the dough to room temperature. Preheat the oven to 400°F.

Roll out the dough on a lightly floured work surface, then use to line the tart pans. Prick the bases and chill or freeze for 15 minutes. Bake blind following the method given on page 19.

Turn the oven down to 325°F. Beat the egg yolks and 6 tablespoons of the sugar with an electric beater until the mixture is pale and mousse-like, and leaves a trail when the beaters are lifted. Beat in the lemon or lime zest and juice. Set the bowl over a saucepan of simmering water and stir the mixture until thickened enough to coat the back of a wooden spoon. Let cool.

Beat the egg whites with the salt until soft peaks form, then gradually beat in the remaining sugar, a spoonful at a time. Beat a spoonful of the egg white mixture into the lemon mixture to loosen it, then carefully fold in the remainder.

Put a single layer of blueberries into each pie crust. Carefully cover with spoonfuls of the lemon mousse, making sure the mousse seals the edges. Put onto the baking sheet and bake for 15–20 minutes until beginning to rise. Dust with confectioners' sugar and return to the oven for 4–5 minutes until just beginning to brown.

Serve warm (the tartlets will sink a little) or at room temperature with spoonfuls of sour cream or crème fraîche and extra blueberries.

blueberry and lime
sour cream pie

1 recipe Pâte Brisée (page 24)

1¼ cups sour cream

2 tablespoons freshly squeezed
lime juice

2 tablespoons Drambuie or other
whiskey liqueur

½ cup sugar

¼ teaspoon ground cinnamon

¼ teaspoon ground allspice

a pinch of salt

2 extra-large eggs, beaten

1 lb. fresh blueberries (3 cups)

½ cup lime marmalade

*a deep tart pan,
9 inches diameter, 1 inch deep*

foil or parchment paper and baking beans

serves 6

The combination of blueberries and lime is terrific, especially when laced with the herby notes of Drambuie. I first tasted wild blueberries sprinkled with Drambuie while fishing in the lochs of Scotland—it was manna from heaven.

Bring the dough to room temperature. Preheat the oven to 400°F.

Roll out the dough thinly on a lightly floured work surface, then use to line the tart pan. Prick the base, then chill or freeze for 15 minutes. Bake blind following the method on page 19.

Turn the oven down to 350°F. Put the sour cream, lime juice, Drambuie or other whiskey liqueur, sugar, spices, salt, and eggs into a bowl and mix well. Arrange a single layer of blueberries in the pie crust and pour in the sour cream mixture.

Put the baking sheet into the oven to heat. Bake the tart on the preheated sheet for 45 minutes until the filling is set and the crust cooked. Remove from the oven and let cool. Remove from the tart pan.

Melt the marmalade and, when runny, push through a strainer. Mix the rest of the blueberries with the marmalade and pile on top of the cooled pie. Chill for at least 1 hour, but remove from the refrigerator 15 minutes before serving.

strawberry chocolate tarts

I make these for special teatime treats in the summer when Scottish strawberries are in season. They beat anything you can buy at the baker or supermarket. Brushing the inside of the pie crusts with chocolate keeps the crust crisp and adds a new dimension to the traditional strawberry tart.

1 recipe Sweet Rich Shortcrust Pastry Dough (page 14, see note)

8 oz. bittersweet chocolate, to make swirls and brush the pie crusts

mascarpone filling

8 oz. mascarpone cheese (1 cup)

2 tablespoons sugar

8 oz. fromage frais or cream cheese, such as Philadelphia (1 cup)

rose water or Grand Marnier, to taste

strawberry topping

12 large, ripe strawberries

red currant jelly, for brushing

a cookie cutter, 4 inches diameter

12 deep fluted tart or brioche pans, 3 inches diameter

nonstick parchment paper

makes 12 small deep tarts

Bring the dough to room temperature. Preheat the oven to 375°F.

Roll out the dough as thinly as possible on a lightly floured work surface, then cut out 12 circles with the cookie cutter. Use these to line 6 of the tart or brioche pans.

Trim the edges and prick the bases. Then set another pan inside each one—this will weight down the dough while it is baking. Chill or freeze for 15 minutes. Bake blind for 10–12 minutes until golden and set. Remove the inner pans and return to the oven to dry out for 5 minutes. Cool, then remove from the outer pans. Repeat with the remaining dough to make another 6.

Melt the chocolate and sprinkle spoonfuls randomly from a height onto nonstick parchment paper. Let cool until set. Use the remaining chocolate to brush the insides of the tarts, making sure they are completely covered. Let cool and set.

To make the filling, put the mascarpone and sugar into a bowl and beat until creamy, then beat in the fromage frais or cream cheese. Add rosewater or Grand Marnier to taste.

Spoon this mixture into the tartlets, filling well, then set a nice fat strawberry on top. Melt the red currant jelly, cool slightly, then brush over the strawberries and the exposed mascarpone surface. Set aside in a cool place to set.

To serve, break up the set chocolate swirls and push a shard into each tart. Serve immediately.

Really ripe strawberries nestling on top of a vanilla pastry cream scented with orange flower water and smothered in red currant jelly—the taste of summer in a tart! Pâte sucrée is the ideal pastry here, since it bakes to a sweet crispness and doesn't go soggy. Rather than using melted red currant jelly for the glaze, I've made a strawberry sauce with gelatin, which will stay set for some time.

classic strawberry vanilla tart

1 recipe Pâte Sucrée (page 26)

1 lb. evenly sized ripe strawberries

vanilla crème pâtissière

4 large egg yolks

1/3 cup sugar

3 tablespoons all-purpose flour

1 vanilla bean

1 1/4 cups milk

2 tablespoons orange flower water or kirsch

strawberry glaze

3 oz. strawberries, sliced (about 3/4 cup)

1 tablespoon sugar

1/2 teaspoon powdered gelatin

a rectangular false-bottom tart pan, 14 x 4 1/2 inches, or a round false-bottom tart pan, 10 inches diameter

foil or parchment paper and baking beans

serves 6

Bring the dough to room temperature. Preheat the oven to 375°F.

Roll out the dough thinly on a lightly floured work surface, then use to line the tart pan. Prick the base, then chill or freeze for 15 minutes.

Line with foil and baking beans and bake blind for 15 minutes. Remove the foil and beans, turn the oven down to 350°F, and return to the oven for 10–15 minutes to dry out and brown. Let cool, then remove from the pan and set on the serving platter.

Meanwhile, to make the crème pâtissière, put the egg yolks and sugar into a bowl and beat until pale and thick. Beat in the flour. Cut the vanilla bean in half lengthwise and scrape out the tiny black seeds. Beat the seeds into the milk, bring to a boil, then pour onto the egg mixture, beating all the time. Return to the pan and slowly bring to a boil, stirring constantly. Cook gently for 2–3 minutes (it doesn't matter if it boils), then beat in the orange flower water and pour into the pie crust. Level the surface and let cool completely.

To make the strawberry glaze, put the sliced strawberries, sugar, and 5 tablespoons water into a small saucepan and simmer for 5 minutes until soft. Blend or strain to make a purée. Sprinkle the gelatin over 2 tablespoons water in a small bowl. Heat the bowl over a saucepan of simmering water until the gelatin has dissolved, then stir into the purée. Let cool until just beginning to set and thicken.

While the glaze is cooling, slice the 1 lb. strawberries thinly and arrange on top of the cold vanilla cream. Spoon or brush the cooled glaze over the strawberries and chill for at least 1 hour to set. Serve cool, but not refrigerator cold.

A tart that celebrates the perfect marriage of raspberries and cream. This is simplicity itself to make, but must be assembled at the last moment to keep the freshness and crispness of the crust. I like to sweeten the cream with a little strained homemade raspberry jam and I add a dash of framboise (raspberry liqueur) if I have it.

fresh raspberry tart

1 recipe Pâte Brisée (page 24)

2–3 tablespoons homemade raspberry jam

2³/₄ cups heavy cream, or 1¹/₄ cups heavy cream mixed with 1¹/₄ cups crème fraîche or sour cream

2 tablespoons framboise, (optional)

1¹/₂ lb. fresh raspberries (5 cups)

1¹/₄ cups raspberry or red currant jelly (any berry preserves will do)

a false-bottom fluted tart pan, 8 inches diameter

foil or parchment paper and baking beans

serves 6–8

Bring the dough to room temperature. Preheat the oven to 400°F.

Roll out the dough thinly on a lightly floured work surface, and use to line the tart pan. Prick the base, chill or freeze for 15 minutes, then bake blind following the method given on page 19. Let cool.*

Press the raspberry jam through a strainer to remove the seeds, then put into a large bowl. Add the cream and framboise, if using. Beat until thick and just holding peaks. Spoon into the pie curst and level the surface. Cover with the raspberries, arranging a final neat layer on top.

Put the raspberry or red currant jelly into a small saucepan and warm it gently until liquid. Brush over the raspberries to glaze.** Put into the refrigerator to chill and set for 10 minutes only before serving (no longer or the tart will go soggy).

***Note** You may like to brush the inside of the pie crust with melted white chocolate before filling—this will keep the crust crisp, and make the tart even more of a special treat! You could also decorate the top with white chocolate curls (use a chocolate with a low cocoa solid content, bring it to room temperature, and shave with a potato peeler).

Variation I sometimes lightly toss the raspberries in the jelly (you may need a bit extra jelly to do this), coating them completely without breaking them. I then spoon them over the surface in a higgledy-piggledy fashion.

Another French pâtisserie classic. The secret of this tart is patience and neatness because it just has to look beautiful! Make it with the juiciest apples you can—Golden Delicious are very good. The pastry provides a firm, crisp support. Unsweetened pâte brisée is used here, because the tart has to be baked for a long time and pastries with a high sugar content would scorch before the apples were cooked.

tarte aux pommes
(French apple tart)

1 recipe Pâte Brisée (page 24)

apple filling

4–5 well-flavored eating apples, peeled and cored

3 tablespoons sugar

4 tablespoons unsalted butter, cubed

4–6 tablespoons apricot jam

2 tablespoons Calvados (apple brandy) or brandy

a false-bottom tart pan, 10 inches diameter

a baking sheet

a wire rack

serves 6–8

Bring the dough to room temperature. Preheat the oven to 400°F and put a baking sheet in the oven to heat.

Roll out the dough thinly on a lightly floured work surface and use to line the tart pan. Chill or freeze for 15 minutes.

Meanwhile, slice the apples thinly, and coarsely chop the uneven smaller pieces. Arrange these smaller pieces in the base of the tart. Cover with one-third of the slices any way you like. Arrange the remaining slices neatly in concentric rings over the chopped apples. Sprinkle with the sugar and dot with the butter.

Set the tart pan on the baking sheet and bake at for about 1 hour until the apples are very well browned and the crust golden. Remove from the oven and transfer to a wire rack. Wait for 5 minutes, then remove the tart pan.

Put the apricot jam and Calvados into a small saucepan and warm gently. Strain, then use to glaze the apples. Serve at room temperature.

This familiar favorite is easy to make—and a must for anyone with a young family. The fruit filling is not too spicy, and children will love the crumble topping.

lemony apple crumble tart

1 recipe Basic Shortcrust Pastry Dough (page 13) or Sweet Rich Shortcrust Pastry Dough (page 14, see note)

vanilla ice cream or custard, for serving

crumble topping

½ cup all-purpose flour

⅓ cup light brown sugar

6 tablespoons unsalted butter, softened

finely grated zest of 1 unwaxed lemon

spiced apple filling

6 large apples, such as Granny Smiths, peeled and cored

2 oz. golden raisins (⅓ cup)

finely grated zest and juice of 1 unwaxed lemon

¼ cup light brown sugar

½ teaspoon cinnamon

½ teaspoon nutmeg

1 tablespoon each all-purpose flour and sugar, mixed

a tart pan, 9 inches diameter

foil or parchment paper and baking beans

serves 6

Bring the dough to room temperature. Preheat the oven to 400°F, or 375°F if using Sweet Rich Shortcrust Pastry Dough.

Roll out the dough on a lightly floured work surface, and use to line the tart pan. Prick the base, then chill or freeze for 15 minutes. Bake blind following the method given on page 19. Let cool.

To make the topping, put the flour, sugar, butter, and lemon zest into a bowl and rub lightly between your fingers until the mixture resembles fine bread crumbs. Chill in the refrigerator until needed.

To make the apple filling, chop the apples into small chunks, put into a bowl and toss with the golden raisins, lemon zest and juice, brown sugar, and spices. Sprinkle the base of the pie crust with the flour and sugar, then arrange the apples on top.

Sprinkle the crumble mixture over the apples. Bake for 15 minutes, then reduce the oven temperature to 350°F and bake for another 30 minutes. Serve warm with vanilla custard.

A tart named after the sisters who, as legend has it, created an upside-down apple tart by mistake! The type of apple used is crucial here—it must retain its shape during cooking and yet have a good flavor. I like to use Golden Delicious or Jonagolds.

tarte des demoiselles tatin

1 recipe Rough Puff Pastry Dough (page 35) or Cheat's Rough Puff Pastry Dough (page 39) or 1 lb. frozen puff pastry, thawed

1¼ cups sugar

1½ sticks chilled unsalted butter, thinly sliced

4½–5 lb. evenly sized dessert apples

crème fraîche or whipped cream, to serve

nonstick parchment paper

a baking sheet

a cast-iron skillet or tarte tatin dish, 11 inches diameter

serves 6

Preheat the oven to 375°F.

Roll out the dough on nonstick parchment paper to a circle about 12 inches in diameter, slide onto a baking sheet, and chill. Sprinkle the sugar over the base of the skillet or tarte tatin dish. Cover with the sliced butter.

Peel, halve, and core the apples. Add the apple halves to the outside edge of the pan: set the first one at an angle, almost on its edge, then arrange the others all around the edge so that they slightly overlap and butt up against each other. Add another ring of apples inside, so that the pan is almost filled, then put a whole half to fill the gap in the center. The apples should now cover the entire surface of the pan. They look awkward and bulky, but will cook down and meld together later.

Put the pan over gentle heat and cook for about 45 minutes until the sugar and butter have caramelized and the apples have softened underneath. (Check every now and then and adjust the heat if necessary. The juices will gradually bubble up the sides; keep cooking until they are a dark amber.)

Lay the dough over the apples in the pan and tuck the edges down into the pan, making the rim of the tart. Prick the top of the dough here and there with a fork, then set the pan on the baking sheet. Bake for 25–30 minutes until the pastry is risen and golden.

Remove the pan from the oven and immediately invert the tart onto a warm serving plate (watch out for hot caramel). Replace any apple slices that stick to the pan. Serve warm, not hot, with crème fraîche or whipped cream.

What could be better than the simplicity of pears poached in red wine? This tart is! The pears absorb the deep flavor of the wine and turn a fabulously rich color. If you want to be outrageously extravagant, use Italian Vin Santo or Marsala instead of red wine and cut down on the sugar—the pears will turn a beautiful dark mahogany.

drunken pear tart

1 recipe Pâte Brisée (page 24) or Cheat's Rough Puff Pastry Dough (page 39)

8 large under-ripe pears

1 cinnamon stick

$1/3$ cup sugar

$2^{3}/4$ cups full-bodied red wine

slivered pistachios or almonds, for sprinkling

crème fraîche or whipped cream, for serving

a cast-iron skillet, 11 inches diameter

serves 6

If using Pâte Brisée, bring to room temperature before rolling out.

Peel the pears, halve lengthwise, and carefully scoop out the core with a teaspoon or melon baller. Arrange them around the base of the skillet in concentric circles, wide ends outwards and the points facing into the center. Any pears remaining should be cut up and used to fill any gaps.

Crumble the cinnamon over the top and sprinkle with the sugar. Carefully pour in the red wine, then bring to a boil. Cover and simmer gently for about 1 hour or until tender.

Preheat the oven to 400°F. Uncover the pan and hold a plate or pan lid over the pears to hold them back while you pour off the juices into a saucepan. Boil the juices hard until well reduced and syrupy, then sprinkle them back over the pears.

Roll out the dough on a lightly floured work surface to a circle slightly larger than the diameter of the pan. Lift the dough over the pears and tuck the edge of the dough down into the pan. Bake for 35–40 minutes, until the crust is crisp and golden.

As soon as it is ready, invert the tart onto a plate or it will stick—the fruit will be very hot, so be careful you don't burn your fingers. Serve warm or at room temperature, sprinkled with the pistachios or almonds and a good deal of crème fraîche or whipped cream.

free-form caramelized peach tart

1 recipe Puff Pastry Dough (page 29), Rough Puff Pastry Dough (page 35) or Cheat's Rough Puff Pastry Dough (page 39)

4–6 ripe peaches

5 tablespoons butter

freshly squeezed juice of ½ lemon

1 cup sugar

whipped cream or crème fraîche, to serve

a dinner plate, 11 inches diameter (to use as a template)

a baking sheet

serves 6

The original version of this tart is sold at my local pâtisserie in France. Monsieur Demont makes all his own pastry on the premises, and when peaches are in season and at their best, these tarts appear in the window in all their rustic glory. So simple and so good—especially with homemade all-butter pastry.

Preheat the oven to 450°F.

Roll out the dough on a lightly floured work surface and cut out a circle, 11 inches in diameter, using a large dinner plate as a template. Lift onto a baking sheet and make an edge by twisting the dough over itself all the way around the edge. Press lightly to seal. Chill or freeze, still on the baking sheet, for at least 15 minutes.

Peel the peaches if necessary, then halve and pit them and cut into chunky slices. Put the butter into a saucepan, then add the lemon juice and half the sugar. Heat until melted, then add the peaches and toss gently. Pile the peaches all over the dough in a casual way. Sprinkle with the remaining sugar and bake in the preheated oven for 20–25 minutes, until golden, puffed and caramelized. Serve with whipped cream or crème fraîche.

A classic of the French pâtisserie—thin crisp pastry filled with a thin layer of golden custard and topped with soft, musky apricots, glistening with apricot jam and their edges just "caught" in the oven. The pie crust is not baked blind beforehand because it would burn.

tarte aux abricots (apricot tart)

1 recipe Pâte Sucrée (page 26) or My Just-Push-It-In Pastry Dough (page 41)

crème pâtissière

5 large egg yolks

½ cup sugar

3 tablespoons all-purpose flour

1¾ cups milk

2 tablespoons kirsch or brandy

apricot topping and glaze

1–1¼ lb. fresh apricots, depending on their size

¼ cup sugar

3 tablespoons apricot jam, for glazing

a little kirsch or brandy

a false-bottom tart pan, 10 inches diameter

a nonstick baking sheet with a rim

a baking sheet

a wire rack

serves 6–8

If using Pâte Sucrée, bring to room temperature before rolling out.

To make the crème pâtissière, put the egg yolks and sugar into a bowl and beat until pale and thick. Beat in the flour. Put the milk into a small saucepan and bring to a boil, then beat into the egg mixture. Return the mixture to the pan and bring to a boil again, stirring constantly. Cook gently for 2–3 minutes. then pour into a bowl and let cool, covering the surface with plastic wrap to prevent a skin from forming.

Roll out the Pâte Sucrée, if using, and line the tart pan. Alternatively, line the pan with My Just-Push-It-In Pastry Dough rounds. Chill for at least 30 minutes.

Preheat the oven to 450°F (or as hot as the oven will go).

Cut the apricots in half and remove the pits. Arrange them cut side down on the rimmed baking sheet and sprinkle with sugar. Bake for 5 minutes until they soften and begin to release their juices. Drain off and reserve the juices.

Turn the oven down to 400°F and put the baking sheet onto the middle shelf to preheat. Beat the 2 tablespoons kirsch into the cooled crème pâtissière and spread over the base of the pie crust. Arrange the apricots closely together, cut side up, over the crème. Set the tart pan on the preheated baking sheet and bake for about 40 minutes, until the apricots color and the tart is a deep golden brown.* Cool for 10 minutes before lifting off the outer ring and transferring to the wire rack to cool completely.

Put the apricot jam into a small saucepan, add the reserved apricot juice and kirsch or brandy to taste, and heat gently until liquid. Strain, then use to glaze the tart. Serve at room temperature, preferably on the day it is made.

***Note** This tart is not baked blind, but setting the tart pan on a preheated baking sheet will help make sure the base cooks quickly and becomes crisp.

The rich buttery brioche dough contains a set golden custard studded with fresh cherries. Serve in thin slices with coffee.

golden custard and cherry brioche tart

brioche pastry dough

2 teaspoons active dry yeast

¼ cup milk, warmed

1 tablespoon sugar

1⅔ cups all-purpose flour, plus extra for dusting

1 teaspoon salt

2 extra-large eggs, at room temperature

2 sticks plus 2 tablespoons unsalted butter, softened

custard and cherry filling

¾ cup milk

½ cup heavy cream

1 vanilla bean, split

2 extra-large eggs, plus 1 egg yolk

½ cup plus 2 tablespoons sugar or vanilla sugar

3 tablespoons all-purpose flour

12 oz. fresh cherries, pitted (1½ cups)

extra beaten egg, for glazing

a rectangular false-bottom tart pan, 13 x 4 inches

serves 6

To make the pastry, dissolve the yeast in the warm milk with a pinch of the sugar. Cover and leave in a warm place for 10 minutes to froth.

Sift the flour into a bowl with the remaining sugar and the salt. Put the eggs into a bowl, beat well, then make a well in the flour and pour in the eggs and the frothy yeast mixture. Mix to a soft elastic dough. Add a little more flour if necessary, but keep the dough quite soft. Work in the softened butter until smooth, shiny, and elastic. The dough will not form a ball at this stage. (If preferred, the whole process can be done easily in a large electric mixer fitted with the paddle attachment.)

Cover and let rise in a warm place for 2–4 hours until doubled in size (or leave overnight in the refrigerator). Punch the dough down with your fist, then wrap and chill until firm enough to roll out—this takes about 30 minutes.

To make the custard, put the milk, cream, and split vanilla bean into a saucepan and heat until until almost boiling. Leave to infuse for 15 minutes. Beat the eggs, egg yolk, and sugar together until pale and creamy. Remove the vanilla bean from the milk and cream mixture.* Beat the flour into the egg mixture, then beat in the milk and cream mixture. Set aside.

Preheat the oven to 400°F. Roll out the dough and use to line the tart pan. Pour in the custard, dot with the cherries, and leave in a warm place to rise for 20 minutes. Bake for 15–20 minutes or until the custard is just starting to set.

Turn the oven down to 325°F. Brush the edges of the pie crust with the beaten egg and bake for 45 minutes longer, until golden and set. Cool in the pan. Serve at room temperature.

*****Note** Wash and dry the bean and put into a sugar jar to make vanilla sugar.

Open jam tarts are made wherever there is a tradition of jam-making—but this one is surely the Queen of Jam Tarts! Use the very best homemade jam you can find—that's what will make this tart. If the hazelnuts are not ground finely enough, grind them in a blender together with the sugar to prevent them from sticking.

linzertorte

(Austrian and German jam tart)

hazelnut pastry dough

1⅓ cups all-purpose flour, plus extra for dusting

½ teaspoon ground cinnamon

½ teaspoon nutmeg

1 teaspoon unsweetened cocoa powder

2 sticks unsalted butter, chilled

7 oz. hazelnuts (1½ cups), very finely ground

1 cup sugar

1 large egg, beaten

2 tablespoons kirsch

to fill and finish

8 oz. top-quality raspberry jam

1 large egg yolk, beaten, to glaze

confectioners' sugar, for dusting (optional)

a plate, 8 inches diameter (to use as a template)

a plain tart pan, 10 inches diameter

a baking sheet

nonstick parchment paper

serves 6

Preheat the oven to 400°F.

Sift all the dry ingredients for the dough into a bowl. Rub in the butter until it resembles fine bread crumbs. Stir in the hazelnuts and sugar, beaten egg, and kirsch. Bring together first with round-bladed knife, then with your hands. Knead lightly into a ball and divide in 2 unequal pieces comprising one-third and two-thirds of the dough. Flatten each slightly and wrap in plastic wrap. Chill in the refrigerator for at least 30 minutes.

Roll out the smaller piece of dough on nonstick parchment paper. Cut a circle the same diameter as the 10-inch tart pan, then cut out an 8-inch inner circle, using the plate as a guide, to give a band about 1 inch wide. Cut 6 more strips of dough 1 inch wide and 10 inches long (you can use a fluted pastry wheel for this). Chill in the refrigerator.

Roll out the larger piece of dough and use to line the base and sides of the tart pan set on the baking sheet. Prick the base all over with a fork. Spread the jam evenly over the base, leaving the edge clear. Then flip the edge of the dough carefully over the jam to form a tiny edge or rim (trim as necessary), as shown on page 22. Freeze for 15 minutes if the dough is getting very soft.

Brush the rim of the tart base with a little water and set the 6 dough strips in a lattice pattern over the jam. Brush the edges with a little more water, then lay the circular band on top, gently press to seal and trim where necessary.

Brush the pastry top with the beaten egg and bake for about 20 minutes or until firm and golden. Cool and remove from the pan. Fill up any deep holes with more jam, and serve at room temperature, dusted with confectioners' sugar, if using. The linzertorte may be kept in an airtight container for up to 2 weeks.

cranberry cinnamon crunch tart

streusel pastry dough

2½ sticks butter, softened, plus extra for the pan

¼ cup sugar

2 tablespoons safflower oil

1 teaspoon vanilla extract

1 large egg

3 cups all-purpose flour, plus extra for dusting

1 teaspoon baking powder

¼ teaspoon salt

2 teaspoons ground cinnamon

cranberry sauce

12 oz. fresh or frozen cranberries, 3 cups

⅔ cup sugar

grated zest and juice of 1 orange

to finish

⅓ cup light brown sugar

confectioners' sugar, for dusting

a springform cake pan, 10 inches diameter

nonstick parchment paper

serves 12

A delightful cross between a cookie and a cake. The light almost shortbread pastry has a layer of thick cranberry sauce in the middle, providing a sharp contrast to its butteriness. Delicious cut into thin wedges and served with coffee.

To make the cranberry sauce, put the cranberries and sugar into a food processor and chop coarsely. Transfer to saucepan and add the orange zest and juice. Bring to a boil, stirring constantly. Simmer for 5 minutes, then set aside to cool completely.

To make the streusel dough, cream the butter and sugar in a bowl until light and fluffy. Beat in the safflower oil and vanilla extract. Lightly beat the egg and beat into the mixture. Sift the flour, baking powder, salt, and cinnamon together into a second bowl. Gradually stir into the first bowl until the dough resembles a coarse shortbread mixture. Bring the dough together with your hands and knead lightly into a ball. Wrap and chill for 2 hours or until very firm.

Line the base of the cake pan with the nonstick parchment paper. Butter and flour the sides of the pan. When the dough is thoroughly chilled, remove from the refrigerator and unwrap. Divide into 2 and wrap the piece you are not using immediately and return it to the refrigerator.

Grate the first half of the dough coarsely into the pan to cover the base evenly. Do not pack down. Carefully spoon in the cold cranberry sauce, avoiding the edges. Remove the remaining dough from the refrigerator and grate evenly over the top, then sprinkle thickly with the brown sugar. Bake at 300°F for about 1¼–1½ hours, until pale but firm.

Cool in the pan, then remove the tart from the pan. Dust with confectioners' sugar to serve. The tart may be stored in an airtight container for up to 1 week.

Fresh dates are so sweet and sticky, they make a fantastic quick-and-easy topping for a crisp puff pastry base. The maple syrup and sugar caramelize with the butter and give the tarts a wonderful sheen. Don't serve them too hot, or you will burn your mouth.

sticky date flaky tarts
with caramel oranges

1 recipe Puff Pastry Dough (page 29), Rough Puff Pastry Dough (page 35) or Cheat's Rough Puff Pastry Dough (page 39)

caramel oranges

4 small, juicy, thin-skinned oranges

1/2 cup plus 2 tablespoons sugar

date topping

6 tablespoons butter

3 tablespoons light brown sugar

2 tablespoons maple syrup

12–16 fresh dates, such as Medjool

3 oz. walnut pieces (3/4 cup)

a saucer or similar, 5 inches diameter (to use as a template)

a large baking sheet

serves 4

Preheat the oven to 400°F.

Roll out the dough thinly on a lightly floured work surface, then cut out 4 circles, 5 inches diameter, using the saucer as a guide. Transfer to a large baking sheet, prick all over with a fork, then chill or freeze for 15 minutes.

To make the caramel oranges, slice the top and bottom off each orange, then cut off the skin in a spiral, as if you were peeling an apple. Try to remove all the bitter white pith. Slice down between the membranes and flick out each segment. Catch the juice in a bowl, then squeeze the remaining juice out of the membrane "skeletons."

Put the sugar and 3 tablespoons water into a heavy saucepan. Cook over low heat until the sugar has completely dissolved and the liquid is clear. Increase the heat and boil until the liquid turns a dark caramel color. Quickly remove the pan from the heat, stand back, and add another 3 tablespoons water—it will hiss and splutter.

Return the pan to low heat and stir until all the hardened pieces of caramel have dissolved. Pour in the reserved orange juice and boil hard until very thick and syrupy. Remove from the heat and let cool completely before adding the orange segments. Chill until needed.

To make the date topping, cut the dates in half and remove the pits. Put the butter, brown sugar, and maple syrup into a saucepan and melt over gentle heat, then add the dates and walnuts.

Spoon the mixture over the circles, leaving a small clear rim on the outside of each. Bake for 15–18 minutes until the pastry is risen and golden and the dates sizzling. Serve with the caramel oranges.

My grandmother made wonderful tartlets in muffin pans and let me fill them with bright yellow store-bought lemon curd. I don't know if she would approve of these exotic mouthfuls— they are very wicked. Remember, the more wrinkled the passionfruit, the riper the flesh inside. Why not make double the quantity of curd and store any you don't use?

pineapple and passionfruit curd tartlets

1 recipe Pâte Sucrée (page 26)

passionfruit curd

6 ripe, juicy passionfruit

freshly squeezed juice of 1 small lemon, strained

6 tablespoons butter, cubed

3 extra-large eggs, beaten

1¼ cups sugar

fruit topping

1 small fresh pineapple, peeled, cored, and sliced

4 passionfruit

a fluted cookie cutter, 3 inches diameter

a 12-cup muffin pan

foil or parchment paper and baking beans

makes 12 tartlets

Bring the dough to room temperature before rolling out.

Cut the 6 passionfruit in half, scoop out the flesh, and press through a strainer into a large bowl to extract the juice. Add the lemon juice, butter, eggs, and sugar and set over a saucepan of simmering water (or cook in a double boiler). Cook, stirring all the time, for about 20 minutes or until the curd has thickened considerably. If you are brave enough, you can cook this over direct heat, watching that it doesn't get too hot and curdle. Strain into a bowl and set aside.

Preheat the oven to 350°F. Roll out the dough thinly on a lightly floured work surface and cut out 12 rounds with the cookie cutter. Line the muffin tin with the dough, pressing it into the cups. Prick the bases and chill or freeze for 15 minutes. Bake blind for 5–6 minutes without lining with beans. Let cool.

When ready to serve, fill the tartlet crusts with a spoonful of passionfruit curd, then top with sliced pineapple. Cut the 4 passionfruit in half, scoop out the flesh and spoon a little, seeds and all, over each tartlet. Serve immediately, before the tartlets have a chance to go soggy.

This is an outrage of a tart! Clouds of gooey pavlova meringue float on top of a luscious filling of sliced fresh mango. Lime is the natural partner for mango, enhancing the wonderful exotic taste.

mango pavlova tart with lime sauce

1 recipe either Pâte Brisée (page 24) or Pâte Sucrée (page 26)

1 large egg, beaten, to glaze

1 tablespoon flour mixed with 1 tablespoon sugar

2–3 ripe mangoes, peeled

pavlova topping

4 extra large egg whites

a pinch of salt

1 cup plus 1 tablespoon sugar

1 teaspoon cornstarch

1 teaspoon vanilla extract

1 teaspoon vinegar

lime sauce

finely grated zest and juice of 3 large unwaxed limes

2 tablespoons dark rum

4–6 tablespoons sugar, to taste

a deep tart pan, 9 inches diameter

foil or parchment paper and baking beans

serves 6

Bring the dough to room temperature. Preheat the oven to 400°F if using Pâte Brisée, or 375°F if using Pâte Sucrée.

Roll out the dough thinly on a lightly floured work surface, then use to line the tart pan. Prick with a fork, then chill or freeze for 15 minutes.

If using Pâte Brisée, bake blind following the method given on page 19. If using Pâte Sucrée, line with aluminum foil or parchment paper and baking beans, then bake blind for 15 minutes. Remove the foil or paper and beans, turn the oven down to 350°F, and return to the oven for 10–15 minutes to dry out and brown.

Brush the inside of the tart with the beaten egg and return to the oven for 5–10 minutes until the egg glaze has cooked. Brush and bake again if necessary. Let cool, then sprinkle with the flour and sugar mixture. Lower the oven temperature to 275°F.

Cut the mangoes down each side of the pit and slice the flesh. Arrange the mango slices over the base of the crust.

To make the pavlova topping, put the egg whites and salt into a bowl and beat until very stiff. Gradually beat in the sugar, one large spoonful at a time— making sure that the meringue is "bouncily" stiff before adding the next spoonful. Beat in the cornstarch, vanilla, and vinegar.

Spoon the meringue mixture over the crust, making sure that you seal the edges. Pile the mixture as high as you can. Bake for about 45 minutes until just turning palest brown.

While the tart is cooking, make the lime sauce. Put the lime zest and juice, rum, and sugar into a small saucepan and heat until the sugar melts. Boil for 1 minute, then pour into a small pitcher and let cool.

Remove the tart from the oven, cool slightly, then serve with the lime sauce.

My Scottish-Canadian cousin, Deirdre, introduced us to this pie when living with us in Scotland for a while, back in the 1960s. It seemed so exotic in the far north of Britain—none of us having even seen a pumpkin before, never mind cans of purée—and has remained a family favorite ever since.

pumpkin pie

1 recipe American Pie Crust Dough
(page 16)

pumpkin filling

2 cups homemade pumpkin purée
or one 15 oz. can*

1/2 cup light brown sugar

3 extra large eggs

3/4 cup evaporated milk, about 7 oz.

1/2 cup light corn syrup

a good pinch of salt

1 teaspoon cinnamon

1/2 teaspoon nutmeg

1 teaspoon vanilla extract

2 tablespoons rum (optional)

*2 tart pans or pie plates,
9 inches diameter*

foil or parchment paper and baking beans

makes two 9-inch pies

*To make the purée, cut a pumpkin or butternut squash into large chunks and bake for about 1 hour at 325°F. Scrape the flesh from the skin and purée until smooth in a food processor.

Bring the dough to room temperature. Preheat the oven to 375°F.

Roll out the dough thinly on a lightly floured work surface, then use to line the 2 tart pans or pie plates. Trim and crimp or decorate the edges as you wish (see page 23). Prick the bases all over with a fork, chill or freeze for 15 minutes, then bake blind following the method given on page 19.

Lower the oven to 325°F.

Put all the filling ingredients into a food processor and blend until smooth. Pour into the pie crusts, set on a baking sheet and bake for about 1 hour or until just set. Remove from the oven and let stand for 10 minutes, then remove the tart pan and let cool for a few minutes. Serve warm or at room temperature, not chilled.

Treacle tart in England is made with golden syrup, white bread crumbs, and lemon juice. In Scotland, we use real black treacle, a bit like molasses, in lots of our baking, so I've adapted this tart to be made with molasses as well as pumpernickel (German rye bread) bread crumbs and lime juice. The pumpernickel gives it a wonderful texture. The bananas just have to be there!

real treacle tart
with caramelized bananas

½ recipe Sweet Rich Shortcrust Pastry Dough (page 14, see note)*

5 tablespoons treacle or dark molasses

5 tablespoons golden syrup or light corn syrup

finely grated zest and juice of 1 large unwaxed lime

½ teaspoon freshly grated ginger (optional but recommended)

4 oz. pumpernickel crumbs (use a food processor to make the crumbs)

ice cream, cream, or sour cream, to serve

caramelized bananas

2 large bananas

6 tablespoons unsalted butter

3 tablespoons light brown sugar

a squeeze of fresh lemon juice

a pie plate, 8 inches diameter

serves 4–6

*Make the full recipe, then freeze the remainder for later use.

Bring the dough to room temperature. Preheat the oven to 375°F.

On a lightly floured work surface, roll out the dough to a thickness of ⅛ inch. Use to line the pie plate and prick the base. Make a traditional decorative edge following the method given for the Devil Edge on page 23. Chill or freeze the dough for 15 minutes.

Put the treacle or molasses and golden syrup or light corn syrup into a saucepan, add the lime juice and zest, and ginger, if using, and heat until just warm and runny. Stir in the pumpernickel crumbs. Spread into the pie crust and bake for about 30 minutes or until the filling is just set and the crust is browning at the edges.**

Meanwhile, peel the bananas and cut into chunks. Melt the butter in a skillet and add the sugar. Cook for a couple of minutes until the sugar melts, then turn up the heat and cook until it caramelizes. Add the bananas and toss well to coat with the juices. Sauté over a medium heat until starting to color and smelling delicious. Squeeze in some lemon juice, and remove from the heat.

Cool the tart slightly before serving warm with the bananas and ice cream, cream or sour cream.

Note Although the tart is not baked blind, slipping it onto a preheated baking sheet will help the base cook quickly and crisply.

There's nothing quite as delicious as a real custard tart. I come from a long line of bakers, and these would be one of our "desert island" luxuries. The nutmeg is the classic flavoring here, but I infuse the milk with fresh bay leaf to add a mysterious musky scent to the custard. Fresh bay leaves should be more widely used in baking—the flavor is like nutmeg, but "greener" and sweeter.

little nutmeg and bay leaf custard tarts

1 recipe Pâte Sucrée (page 26)*

nutmeg and bay leaf custard

2²/₃ cups whole milk

3 fresh (preferably) or dried bay leaves

6 large egg yolks

¹/₃ cup sugar

1 whole nutmeg

8 false-bottom tart pans, 4 inches diameter (or use smaller but deeper pans and increase the cooking time)

2 baking sheets

a wire rack

makes about 8 tarts

*Use any leftover dough to make a few more tarts.

Bring the dough to room temperature. Preheat the oven to 400°F.

Roll out the dough thinly on a lightly floured work surface and use to line the tart pans. Put these on the baking sheet and chill for 30 minutes.

To make the custard, put the milk and bay leaves into a saucepan and heat until lukewarm. Put the egg yolks and sugar into a bowl and beat until pale and creamy. Pour the warmed milk onto the yolks and stir well—do not beat or you will get bubbles. Strain into a small pitcher and pour into the tart cases. Grate fresh nutmeg liberally over the surface of the tartlets.

Preheat the other baking sheet in the oven.** Put the tart pans onto the preheated sheet and bake in the oven for 10 minutes. Lower the heat to 350°F and bake until set and just golden—about another 10 minutes. Don't overbake, as the custard should be a bit wobbly when the tarts come out of the oven.

Remove from the pans and let cool on a wire rack. Serve at room temperature.

**Note Because the tarts are not baked blind, slipping them onto a preheated baking sheet will help the bases cook quickly and crisply.

jacks' rose petal tart

This is the most beautiful and delicious tart in the world. The recipe was given to me by my sister Jacks. It tastes so delicate—and is lovely to serve at a wedding or christening.

1 recipe Puff Pastry Dough (page 29) or 12 oz. frozen puff pastry, thawed*

rose-flavored filling

$1/2$ cup plain yogurt

$1^{1}/2$ cups heavy cream

1 large egg yolk

2–3 tablespoons rose water

2 tablespoons sugar

crystallized rose petals

1 large egg white

superfine sugar

petals of 2–4 scented roses

a wire rack or nonstick parchment paper

foil and baking beans

a heart-shaped or round tart pan, 10 inches diameter

foil or parchment paper and baking beans

makes one 10-inch tart

If using 1 recipe of homemade Puff Pastry, you will have some left over to freeze for later use.

To crystallize the rose petals, put the egg white into a bowl, beat until frothy, then paint onto clean dry petals. Sprinkle with sugar to coat completely, then arrange on a cake rack or nonstick parchment paper and leave in a warm place to dry out and crisp—at least overnight. Cool, but do NOT put into the refrigerator. Store between layers of paper towels in an airtight container.

Preheat the oven to 450°F. Roll out the dough as thinly as possible. Use to line the tart pan, pressing it into the sides and trimming to leave $1/8$ inch hanging over the edge. Turn this inwards to make a rim. Prick the base all over with a fork, then chill or freeze for 15 minutes. Line with foil and baking beans and bake blind for 12–15 minutes. Lower the oven temperature to 400°F, remove the foil and beans, and return to the oven for 5 minutes longer to dry out. You may have to flatten the pastry if it puffs up.

Turn the oven down to 350°F. Put the yogurt, $1/4$ cup of the cream, the egg yolk, rose water, and sugar into a bowl and mix well. Put the remaining cream into a bowl and beat until soft peaks form, then fold into the yogurt mixture. Spoon into the baked pie crust, level the surface, and bake for about 20 minutes. It will seem almost runny, but will set as it cools. Cover and chill until firm.

Decorate with the crystallized rose petals. Serve slightly cold.

Wickedly delicious. Use the darkest chocolate you can find and serve in thin slices. The filling is gooey and rich inside—delicious with a spoonful of sour cherry jam and another of sour cream or crème fraîche. I sometimes spread the base of the tart with the jam before pouring in the mixture.

baked darkest chocolate mousse tart

1 recipe Pâte Sucrée (page 26)

confectioners' sugar, for dusting

chocolate mousse filling

14 oz. bittersweet chocolate, broken into pieces

1¼ sticks unsalted butter, cubed

5 extra-large eggs, separated

½ cup plus 2 tablespoons sugar

⅔ cup heavy cream, at room temperature

3 tablespoons dark rum (optional)

a false-bottom deep tart pan, 10 inches diameter, 1½ inches deep

foil or parchment paper and baking beans

serves 8

Bring the dough to room temperature. Preheat the oven to 375°F.

Roll out the dough thinly on a lightly floured work surface, then use to line the tart pan. Prick the base with a fork, then chill or freeze for 15 minutes.

Line with foil and baking beans and bake blind for 15 minutes. Remove the foil and beans, turn the oven down to 350°F, and return to the oven for 10–15 minutes to dry out and brown. Cool and remove from the pan, then transfer to a serving platter.

Put the chocolate and butter into a bowl and melt over a saucepan of simmering water. As soon as it has melted, remove the bowl from the heat and cool slightly for a minute or so.

Put the egg yolks and sugar into a bowl and beat with electric beaters until pale and creamy. Stir the cream and rum, if using, into the melted chocolate mixture, then quickly fold in the egg yolk mixture. Put the egg whites into a clean bowl and beat until soft peaks form. Quickly fold into the chocolate mixture.

Pour into the pie crust and bake for 25 minutes until risen and a bit wobbly. Remove from the oven and let cool—the filling will sink and firm up as it cools. Dust with confectioners' sugar, and serve at room temperature with cream.

Cardamom adds an exotic aftertaste to this satin-smooth chocolate tart. I wrote this recipe while staying in France. It was spring, and violets were peeping up along the drive to the house. I decided to crystallize them to decorate the tart for the photograph—and here they are—my *violettes de Toulouse*! Gold almond dragées would also look spectacular for a really special occasion!

chocolate and cardamom cream tart

1 recipe My Just-Push-It-In Pastry Dough (page 41) or Pâte Sucrée (page 26)

chocolate and cardamom filling

1¼ cups heavy cream

4 cardamom pods, crushed

8 oz. bittersweet chocolate, broken into pieces

3 tablespoons sugar

to finish

1¼ cups heavy cream

2 pinches of ground cardamom

confectioners' sugar, to taste

crystallized violets*

a tart pan, 8 inches diameter

foil or parchment paper and baking beans

serves 6

*Gather the violets in the morning when they are fresh. Dry them, then paint the petals with just foamy, beaten egg white. Dust with superfine sugar and put onto a wire cake rack in a warm place to dry—at least overnight. They should completely dry out and become brittle and crisp. To store, pack between layers of paper towels in an airtight container.

If using Pâte Sucrée, bring to room temperature. Preheat the oven to 375°F.

Roll out the dough thinly on a lightly floured work surface, then use to line the tart pan. Prick the base with a fork, then chill or freeze for 15 minutes. Line with foil and baking beans and bake blind for 15 minutes. Remove the foil and beans, turn the oven down to 350°F, and return the pie crust to the oven for 10–15 minutes to dry out and brown. Cool and remove from the pan, then transfer to a serving platter.

If using My Just-Push-It-In Pastry Dough, line the pan with the dough rounds. Chill or freeze for 15 minutes, then bake blind following the method given on page 19. Let cool, then remove from the pan and transfer to a serving platter.

Put the cream and cardamom pods into a saucepan and heat until almost boiling. Remove from the heat and set aside to infuse for 20 minutes. When the cream is infused, put the chocolate and sugar into a bowl set over a saucepan of simmering water. Strain the infused cream over the chocolate and stir occasionally until melted.

Remove from the heat and let cool. Watch it carefully—just as it begins to thicken and set, start beating with an electric beater. Beat for 5 minutes until thick and light, then pour into the pie crust. Let set.

To finish, whip the cream, and flavor with the ground cardamom and confectioners' sugar, to taste. Decorate the tart as you like, with the whipped cardamom cream and the crystallized violets.

This recipe comes from Carl, the chef who cooked for us in a chalet in Méribel, France, during a skiing holiday. He was a fabulous cook and a dream of a pastry chef—this is one of his specialties.

carl's chocolate pecan tart with coffee bean sauce

1 recipe Sweet Rich Shortcrust Pastry Dough (page 14, see note) or Pâte Sucrée (page 26)

1 large egg, beaten, for glazing

chocolate filling

4 oz. bittersweet chocolate

4 tablespoons unsalted butter

3 extra-large eggs, beaten

¾ cup maple syrup

8 oz. pecans (about 1 cup)

coffee bean sauce

1 vanilla bean, split lengthwise

1¼ cups milk

1 tablespoon finely ground espresso coffee

1 tablespoon sugar

2 large egg yolks

2 tablespoons Cognac or Armagnac

a tart pan, 10 inches diameter

foil or parchment paper and baking beans

serves 6

Bring the dough to room temperature. Preheat the oven to 375°F.

If using Sweet Rich Shortcrust Pastry Dough, roll out on a lightly floured work surface and use to line the tart pan. Prick the base and chill or freeze for 15 minutes. Bake blind following the method on page 19. Glaze with beaten egg and bake again for 5–10 minutes. Let cool.

If using Pâte Sucrée, bring to room temperature. Roll out the dough thinly on a lightly floured work surface, then use to line the tart pan. Prick the base, then chill or freeze for 15 minutes. Line with foil and baking beans and bake blind for 15 minutes. Remove the foil and beans, turn the oven down to 350°F and return to the oven for 10–15 minutes to dry out and brown. Glaze with the beaten egg and bake again for 5–10 minutes. Let cool.

To make the chocolate filling, lower the oven temperature to 325°F. Break up the chocolate and put it into the top of a double boiler or a bowl set over a saucepan of simmering water. Add the butter and stir over gentle heat until melted. Put the eggs and maple syrup into a bowl and beat well. Add to the chocolate. Stir well, and keep stirring over low heat until the mixture starts to thicken. Stir in the pecans and pour into the pie crust.

Bake for 35–40 minutes, until just set—the filling will still be a bit wobbly.

Meanwhile, to make the sauce, put the vanilla bean, milk, coffee, and sugar into a saucepan and heat gently. Bring almost to a boil, then set aside to infuse for 15 minutes. Remove the vanilla bean*.

Put the egg yolks into a bowl, beat well, then pour in the infused milk. Mix well and return to the pan. Stir with a wooden spoon over gentle heat until the custard coats the back of the spoon. Pour into a cold bowl and stir in the Cognac. Cover with plastic wrap, cool, and chill until needed.

Serve the tart warm with the coffee bean sauce—or with cream.

***Note** Rinse and dry the bean, and store in a sugar jar to make vanilla sugar.

My sister is responsible for this outrageous recipe. We were chatting about brownies one night and she came up with the idea of making a walnut crust for the tart instead of having the nuts in the filling. Here is the result. My niece Cassia helped to stir the mixture for the tart in the photograph—I wonder if there was any ulterior motive in her kind gesture?

double chocolate brownie tart with walnut crust

6 oz. graham crackers

6 oz. walnut halves (1½ cups), coarsely chopped

1¼ sticks unsalted butter, melted

brownie filling

4 oz. bittersweet chocolate, broken into small pieces

1¾ sticks butter

2 cups sugar

3 extra large eggs, beaten

1 teaspoon vanilla extract

1 cup all-purpose flour

8 oz. white chocolate chips (1⅓ cups)

a deep cake pan, 9 inches square

nonstick parchment paper

makes about 16 brownies

Line the base of the pan with a square of nonstick parchment paper to make removing the finished tart easier.

To make the base, crush the crackers and walnuts in a food processor, pulsing to keep the mixture quite coarse. Stir the mixture into the melted butter until evenly coated. Press evenly into the base and 1¾ inches up the sides of the pan (a flat potato masher will help you to do this) before it cools. Chill in the refrigerator for 20 minutes to set the base before filling.

Preheat the oven to 350°F.

To make the filling, put the chocolate into a small bowl and melt over a saucepan of hot water. Put the butter and sugar into a bowl, cream until light and fluffy, then beat in the eggs. Stir in the melted chocolate and vanilla. Fold in the flour, then half the chocolate chips. Spoon into the pie crust and level the top. Sprinkle with the remaining chocolate chips.

Bake for 35 minutes or until a toothpick inserted into the middle reveals fudgy crumbs. Do not overcook.

Cool in the pan. When cool, remove from the pan and cut into 16 pieces.

This soft, sticky tart packed with walnuts is superb served with the easy vanilla ice cream marbled with taffy.

walnut tart

with taffy ice cream

1 recipe Sweet Rich Shortcrust Pastry Dough (page 14, see note)

walnut filling

1¼ sticks unsalted butter, softened

½ cup plus 2 tablespoons light brown sugar

3 extra-large eggs

grated zest and juice of 1 small orange

¾ cup light corn syrup

8 oz. walnut halves (2½ cups), coarsely chopped

a pinch of salt

taffy ice cream

6 oz. taffy

½ cup heavy cream

1 pint best-quality vanilla ice cream, softened

a fluted tart pan, 9 inches diameter

foil or parchment paper and baking beans

serves 6

Bring the dough to room temperature. Preheat the oven to 375°F.

Roll out the dough on a lightly floured work surface and use to line the tart pan. Prick the base, chill or freeze for 15 minutes, then bake blind following the method given on page 19. Cool. Lower the oven to 350°F.

To make the filling, put the butter and sugar into a bowl and cream until light and fluffy. Gradually beat in the eggs, one at a time. Beat the orange zest and juice into the butter and egg mixture. Heat the light corn syrup in a small saucepan until runny, but not very hot. Stir into the butter mixture, then stir in the walnuts and salt.

Pour into the pie crust and bake for 45 minutes until lightly browned and risen. The tart will sink a little on cooling.

While the tart is cooling, make the ice cream. Put the taffy and cream into a small saucepan and stir over medium heat to melt. Cool slightly and stir quickly into the ice cream so that it looks marbled. Put the ice cream back in the freezer until ready to serve.

Serve the tart at room temperature with scoops of the taffy ice cream.

A deliciously moist and almondy tart with a crust of caramelized pine nuts. This is perfect served with coffee or with fresh peaches and apricots.

frangipane pine nut tart

1 recipe Pâte Sucrée (page 26) or My Just-Push-It-In Pastry Dough (page 41)

4 oz. pine nuts (1 cup)

2 tablespoons confectioners' sugar, for dusting

almond filling

4 oz. blanched almonds (^{2}/$_3$ cup)

^{1}/$_2$ cup sugar

1 stick unsalted butter, softened

5 extra-large eggs, beaten

2 tablespoons Marsala or dark rum

a pinch of salt

^{2}/$_3$ cup all-purpose flour

a baking sheet

a false-bottom tart pan, 10 inches diameter

serves 6

If using Pâte Sucrée, bring the dough to room temperature. Preheat the oven to 400°F, then set the baking sheet on the middle shelf.

Roll out the dough thinly on a lightly floured work surface, use to line the tart pan, and prick the base all over. Alternatively, line the pan with My Just-Push-It-In Pastry Dough rounds. Chill or freeze for 15 minutes.

To make the almond filling, put the almonds and sugar into a food processor and grind until the almonds are as fine as possible. Add the butter and blend until creamy. Gradually blend in the beaten eggs, then add the Marsala or rum and the pinch of salt. Finally, add the flour, blending quickly until just mixed.

Spread the filling over the base of the tart, then sprinkle with the pine nuts. Don't worry if there seems to be too little filling—it will rise.

Bake on the preheated baking sheet for about 10 minutes, until the crust begins to brown at the edges, then lower the heat to 350°F and bake for 20 minutes longer until puffed, brown, and set.*

Remove the tart from the oven and turn up the heat to 450°F. Sift the confectioners' sugar over the top in a thin and even layer. Return to the oven for 5 minutes or less, until the sugar melts and caramelizes. (Alternatively, put under a preheated broiler, protecting the edges of the crust with foil, for a couple of minutes until the sugar caramelizes.) Serve warm.

*Note Although the tart is not baked blind, slipping it onto a preheated baking sheet will make the base cook quickly and crisply.

mail order directory

King Arthur Flour Baker's Catalogue
P.O. Box 876
Norwich, Vermont 05055-0876
800-827-6836
www.kingarthurflour.com
A catalog of everything the home baker could ever need.

New York Cake & Baking Distributor
56 West 22nd Street
New York, NY 10010
800-942-2539 (outside NY)
212-675-2253
New York's most beloved baking ingredient and equipment retail store. Call for a catalog ($5 shipping cost).

Bridge Kitchenware
214 East 52nd Street
New York, NY 10022
800-274-3435 (outside NY)
212-688-4200
www.bridgekitchenware.com
Extensive selection of tart pans and baking equipment.

Broadway Panhandler
477 Broome Street
New York, NY 10013
212-966-3434
www.broadwaypanhandler.com
Extensive selection of tart pans and baking equipment.

Sur la Table
1765 6th Avenue South
Seattle, WA 98134
800-243-0852
www.surlatable.com
"Fine equipment for cooks and professional chefs."

Penzeys Spices
P.O. Box 933
Muskego, WI 53150
800-741-7787
www.penzeys.com
The source for all baking spices and extracts.

Chef's Catalog
111 Customer Way
Irving, TX 75039
800-884-2433
www.chefscatalog.com

Dean and Deluca
560 Broadway
New York NY 10012
800-221-7714
www.deandeluca.com

Zingerman's Mail Order
620 Phoenix Drive
Ann Arbor, MI 48108
888-636-8162
www.zingermans.com
Gourmet foods shop with a discriminating mail order service.

Williams-Sonoma
3250 Van Ness Avenue
San Francisco, CA 94109
877-812-6235
www.williamssonoma.com
Online and retail source for fine baking products and equipment.

conversion charts

Weights and measures have been rounded up or down slightly to make measuring easier.

volume equivalents

american	metric	imperial
1 teaspoon	5 ml	
1 tablespoon	15 ml	
¼ cup	60 ml	2 fl.oz.
⅓ cup	75 ml	2½ fl.oz.
½ cup	125 ml	4 fl.oz.
⅔ cup	150 ml	5 fl.oz. (¼ pint)
¾ cup	175 ml	6 fl.oz.
1 cup	250 ml	8 fl.oz.

weight equivalents:

imperial	metric
1 oz.	25 g
2 oz.	50 g
3 oz.	75 g
4 oz.	125 g
5 oz.	150 g
6 oz.	175 g
7 oz.	200 g
8 oz. (½ lb.)	250 g
9 oz.	275 g
10 oz.	300 g
11 oz.	325 g
12 oz.	375 g
13 oz.	400 g
14 oz.	425 g
15 oz.	475 g
16 oz. (1 lb.)	500 g
2 lb.	1 kg

measurements:

inches	cm
¼ inch	5 mm
½ inch	1 cm
¾ inch	1.5 cm
1 inch	2.5 cm
2 inches	5 cm
3 inches	7 cm
4 inches	10 cm
5 inches	12 cm
6 inches	15 cm
7 inches	18 cm
8 inches	20 cm
9 inches	23 cm
10 inches	25 cm
11 inches	28 cm
12 inches	30 cm

oven temperatures:

225°F	110°C	Gas ¼
250°F	120°C	Gas ½
275°F	140°C	Gas 1
300°F	150°C	Gas 2
325°F	160°C	Gas 3
350°F	180°C	Gas 4
375°F	190°C	Gas 5
400°F	200°C	Gas 6
425°F	220°C	Gas 7
450°F	230°C	Gas 8
475°F	240°C	Gas 9

index